Starters, Salads, and Sexy Sides

Starters, Salads, and Sexy Sides

INSPIRING RECIPES
to MAKE EVERY
MEAL *an* OCCASION

Caren McSherry

appetite
by RANDOM HOUSE

Dishes pictured:

i: Sweet Pea, Edamame, and Burrata Salad (page 90)

ii–iii: Clockwise from top: Cauliflower Steaks with Capers and Caramelized Lemon
(page 126); Charred Miso Broccolini with Crispy Garlic Chips (page 134); Diane's Endive,
Radicchio, and Globe Grape Salad (page 110)

iv–v: Clockwise from top: Pita Chips (page 31); Warm Olives with Grilled Lemons (page 12);
Spicy Hummus with Crispy Chickpeas (page 33)

viii: Clockwise from top: Deconstructed Classic American Cobb Salad (page 109);
Warm Maple Bacon Spinach Salad (page 70); Heirloom Tomatoes with Herbed Ricotta
(page 113); Sweet Pea, Edamame, and Burrata Salad (page 90)

2: Clockwise from top: Truffle Parmesan Popcorn (page 35); Mini Halloumi Sliders
(page 56); Flatbread Rolls with Crab and Arugula (page 38)

Appetite by Random House® and colophon are registered trademarks of
Penguin Random House LLC.

Library and Archives Canada Cataloguing in Publication is available upon request.
ISBN: 978-0-147-53059-2
eBook ISBN: 978-0-14-753060-8

Cover and book design: Jennifer Griffiths
Cover and book photography: Janis Nicolay
Printed and bound in China

Published in Canada by Appetite by Random House®,
a division of Penguin Random House Canada Limited.

www.penguinrandomhouse.ca

10 9 8 7 6 5 4 3 2 1

appetite
by RANDOM HOUSE | Penguin
Random
House

This book, in its entirety, is dedicated
to my late mother, Clara McSherry.
She lived her life with a joie de vivre like
no other. I am still trying to keep up!

Contents

Sexy Sides

Staple Recipes

Foreword

by Chef Lynn Crawford

Caren McSherry is truly a Canadian culinary icon. I have had the pleasure to have gotten to know her over the past few years, and I can tell you that she is one of the most passionate, talented, generous, smart, creative, hilarious, life-loving, food-loving people that I have ever met! I truly admire her energy, spirit, creativity, and laughter, and especially her love of food.

Over her exciting career, Caren has surrounded herself with the best of the best, travelling and cooking with many of the finest chefs around the world. She has cooked with the highest quality and most interesting ingredients anyone could dream of. And, in addition to being a knowledgeable and inspiring teacher, she really knows how to throw an incredibly fun, delicious dinner party... with lots of tremendous wine!

Sharing the wonderful world of food with passion and expertise is really what Caren does so brilliantly, and *Starters, Salads, and Sexy Sides* is no exception. In this book, Caren gives us easy-to-follow recipes for that incredible dinner party with lots of friends, that delicious family feast, or that special meal you'll dream about devouring all day.

But what's so great about this particular book is its focus on the components that too many other cookbooks downplay, the parts of a meal that can move it from so-so to spectacular and, most of all, memorable.

Often when we are planning a menu, it is the main—whether grilled rib eye steak, slow-roasted leg of lamb, or pan-seared halibut—that seems to get all of the glory. But here, Caren puts the supporting cast members in the leading role with outstanding and delicious recipes that you can mix and match to create the perfect meal for any and every occasion. *Starters, Salads, and Sexy Sides* is also a gorgeous cookbook to look at, with beautiful photography that will entice you to cook with every page you turn.

What makes me happiest is finding a new cookbook that inspires me to get into my kitchen and start cooking. Everything in this cookbook does just that. It is about the wonderful world of food and why I love it, and I hope you'll enjoy it as much as I do. Thanks Caren—you inspire me!

Introduction

One would think that, by now, with the plethora of cookbooks on our shelves, that none of us really needs another. After 40-plus years in this business, my collection numbers more than 1,000! I love to see them lined up in all their colorful glory. Leafing through the pages can be so inspiring, and in every genre of cookbook there is an abundance of choice. Beautiful baking books from sensational bakers; burger books, beef books, every-which-way-to-cook-chicken books; seafood-galore books, and don't forget the barbecue bibles—all these categories are so adequately and deliciously covered.

So that is why you will find no recipes for mains or desserts in this book. For me, and for most of the cooks I know, the biggest challenge is not what to make for the main course, it's what to serve *with* the main course. When planning a dinner party or a family get-together, the easy decision is whether to serve pork, lamb, fish, poultry, or beef; the dilemma lies in which salad to choose, what side dishes to prepare, and of course, what delicious little starters to make to get the party started. With starters, salads, and sides, the potential to elevate a meal from ordinary to extraordinary, or to transform an occasion from "ho hum" to "hot damn!",

is as simple as following the recipes on the following pages.

My goal with this book is to give you a blueprint. The recipes within are adaptable dishes designed to mix, match, and complement almost any main course. Bite-size starters seem to cause hosts and hostesses the most agony, so I have a generous selection of those, all quick and easy to prepare. The salads I suggest can suit a buffet or can be easily scaled down to attractive single servings. The side dishes work both as individually plated portions for sit-down dinners, or presented on platters for a casual barbecue. There are plenty of choices for diet-specific requirements so you can take care of all your guests. The ingredients and tools sections include all you need to know about any special ingredients and equipment used in the recipes.

The more you cook, the better you get, and be sure to add a bit of your own personality by changing up the plating, adding a different garnish, or adapting the dishes into main courses. Whatever your style, I hope you will find *Starters, Salads, and Sexy Sides* an inspiration that will have you and your guests eating happily ever after. So, tie on your apron and turn up the heat—it's time to eat!

Caren

Exceptional Ingredients

My passion for ingredients is what led me to open my store, the Gourmet Warehouse, an emporium for home cooks, chefs, and foodies. The following are my top picks, for times when I believe that having the very best quality ingredients will really take your cooking to the next level. They are available online (check out www.gourmetwarehouse.ca) or at good gourmet stores.

Balsamic Pearls
These are jelly-like pearls—think caviar—that are made using molecular gastronomy. Simply put, aged balsamic vinegar is combined with agar agar, then held in suspension. When you bite into the pearl, a burst of balsamic is released. These are perfect as a garnish on tomatoes, on vegetables, or anytime you would use balsamic (see page 16).

Balsamic Vinegar
This vinegar is centuries in the making. There is no substitute; your balsamic must be from Modena, Italy, to be the real thing, and the older the better. It ages at the source in the barrel, and as you can guess, the longer it is aged the more expensive it will be.

White Balsamic Vinegar
White balsamic is made with white Trebbiano grapes that are pressed and mixed with white vinegar. Unlike dark balsamic, it is aged in new wood barrels rather than aged, fired barrels, and it is not caramelized. White balsamic is a bit cleaner tasting, more acidic, and is primarily used when you do not want to add color to a dressing or marinade.

Capers
Grown in the Mediterranean basin, capers are all about grading and size. Smallest is best, from "surfine" to "capote." The largest tend to be tough and a little chewy. I like to fry them to make Crispy Capers (page 168); they open up into little flowers and make a perfect garnish for fish and vegetables alike.

Chili Paste
A good chili paste should have an even flavor of chili and garlic. I find that Chinese chili pastes are far too prominent on the garlic side, and that Thai pastes lean too heavily on spicy heat. Côte D'Azur Spice 2.0 Chili Paste is a perfect mix of the two, meeting in the middle for palatable balance.

Dijon Mustard
There are many brands of this mustard on the market, but as long as yours hails from Dijon, the city in which it originated, you are good. This mustard will emulsify dressings, perk up a dull sauce, and bring a little zing to breaded items. Although it comes in both grainy and smooth, whenever Dijon mustard is listed in this book, you can assume to use smooth.

Preserved Lemons
This Middle Eastern/Persian condiment provides a unique elevation of flavor. They are simply lemons preserved in a water, sugar, and salt brine, which infuses them with a distinct taste. It is important to know that you use only the rind, which has all the flavor components, and never the pulp. Scrape away and discard the pulp, then finely chop

the rind to add a wonderful zing to various dishes. They can be purchased at any Middle Eastern deli or good gourmet store.

Roasted Grapeseed Oil

The neutral flavor and high smoke point of this oil make it perfect for stir-fries and sautés. I always reach for grapeseed oil over peanut oil to eliminate the risk of allergies.

Hazelnut Oil

Hazelnut oil provides an elegant alternative to olive oil-based vinaigrettes. The fragrant essence of nuts is a highlight. It must be refrigerated once opened. I like French hazelnut oils best.

Extra Virgin Olive Oil

Extra virgin is a must for salads, dressings, and marinades. There are hundreds of offerings on the market, and the profiles are uniquely different from country to country. Tuscan olive oil, for example, has a peppery finish, whereas a French variety has a soft buttery flavor. Portugal and Spain offer a more rounded grassy oil, depending on the terroir where the olive trees are grown. Everyone has a favorite, so yours will be totally personal.

Toasted Sesame Oil

Only purchase sesame oil that has been toasted; it will indicate so on the label, and it has a golden-brown appearance rather than a clear pale color. Kadoya is one of my preferred brands. Once opened, sesame oil must be refrigerated; it will go rancid if kept at room temperature for more than two days.

Smoked Spanish Paprika

Smoked Spanish paprika, not to be confused with Hungarian paprika (which is not smoked), has been given a DOP designation by the Spanish government to indicate that it meets a distinctive regional standard. The peppers are dried and carefully smoked over special woods indicative of the region. It comes in bittersweet, sweet, and hot, and you can interchange them depending on your taste and preference. If you find the flavor strong, you can use half the amount called for in any of the recipes that follow.

Black Peppercorns

The best black peppercorns are from India, generally from the Malabar Coast. The most robust of all black peppercorns, they are big, bold, and lively. A little goes a long way.

Kosher Salt

Often referred to as the salt of chefs, kosher salt has half the saltiness of supermarket boxed salts. It is a chemical-free, inland-mined salt that is perfect for baking and cooking, and is a must for every kitchen, be it professional or home.

Truffle Salt

Truffle salt is the perfect finish for fries, popcorn, risotto, mushrooms, potatoes, and vegetables. A little goes a long way.

Fleur de Sel

This is the darling of fancy finishing salts. There was once a time when only France produced this highly acclaimed salt, but now many other countries have joined the parade. This special salt is raked from the surface of sun-dried salt beds and then heaped to dry in the hot summer sun. The flavor is impeccable, the texture fine and somewhat moist. It isn't cheap, but the end result is compelling and worth the price.

Chicken Stock

Homemade stock is best, but in the interest of time, many cooks opt for pre-made stock, which you can buy in a carton or as a concentrated paste. If you are purchasing stock, make sure that it has no MSG.

Tools and Equipment

Having too many tools and pieces of equipment can sometimes be overwhelming. There are, however, some things you really do need that aren't just drawer fillers. The following list includes items I like to keep in my kitchen, not only to achieve unique presentations, but more importantly, to make things a bit easier while cooking.

Baking Mats
Baking mats can be used as a replacement for parchment paper, and I consider them a baking necessity. Nothing sticks to them, including sticky ribs or shortbread and sugar cookies. The mats can be used up to 3,000 times. I use Silpat, which are made in France.

Cookie Cutters, Regular and Fluted
Though cookie cutters are available in every shape and size you can imagine, I stick to the round or fluted round shape, which are available in metal or plastic. These are useful for cutting out starter-sized portions for many of the recipes in this book.

Fancy Skewers and Toothpicks
There is an abundance of fancy picks and skewers on the market. Use them to embellish your canapés or to hold sliders together.

Food Processor
Food processors are a true necessity in the kitchen to purée, chop, or make dressings and sauces. Purchase the size that suits your cooking best, though remember that while you can put less in a large bowl, you cannot put more in a small one.

Fry Pans
I have been cooking for over 40 years and Scanpan is the best nonstick brand I have used. Made in Denmark with a special material called Stratanium™, these pans brown, sizzle, and grill with minimal fat.

Hasselback Tray
These are small plastic or wooden trays the size of a large bar of soap that have a divot in the middle, so named as they are useful for making Hasselback Potatoes (page 151). The potato is placed on the tray and then carefully sliced so as not to cut all the way through to the bottom. If you do not have one, you can use a large wooden spoon or two chopsticks instead.

German brand Weck, have unique clamp closures. They are not inexpensive but truly make a statement if you are giving a gift, or if your budget allows. The good news is that they can be reused for things like serving desserts, or around the kitchen as a handy way to shake up salad dressings or store homemade sauces and condiments.

Muffin and Mini Muffin Pans

Not just for muffins! These pans are a great tool for creating small, cute portions, or shaping garnishes such as the Parmesan Tuiles (page 167).

Parchment Paper

Parchment paper is a staple in every kitchen for roasting or baking. The paper prevents things from sticking and does not burn in the oven.

Madeleine Pans

These traditional French shell-shaped cake and cookie trays are necessary for preparing—you guessed it—madeleines. I prefer to purchase the nonstick version, as it makes the removal much easier.

Mason Jars

Large Mason jars are great for layered salads, cocktails, or cold soups in summer. Smaller, more elaborate jars, like those made by the

Silicone Molds

The easiest way to create and maintain special shapes is with silicone molds, which come in all shapes and sizes imaginable. The life of the mold is 3,000 uses, and they can go in the freezer, oven, and dishwasher. The small rectangular shape is perfect for sushi (see page 22), as it is bite-sized and the silicone makes the rice so easy to release.

Southwest Salad Baskets
(page 88)

Clockwise from top: Artichoke, Parmesan, and Cannellini Bean Dip (page 34); Charred Eggplant and Za'atar Dip (page 32); Spicy Hummus with Crispy Chickpeas (page 33)

Starters

Starters, or appetizers as most of us call them, are truly the proverbial pain in the butt. They are often small, tedious, and painstaking to prepare. That said, they are, without a doubt, some of the most fun and interesting foods to eat. Who doesn't love a lively cocktail party with all the cute little bites precariously floating around on pretty platters? The fact that they never really count as a meal, or even a single calorie, is even better!

Oh yes, we all love them, but most of us truly dread the thought of preparing them. So in this chapter I'm giving you plenty of inspiration, with a generous mix of small plates to pass around, savory dips to share, and individual starters for sit-down dinners. Try serving two or three dishes from this section at your next canapé party, like the Really Good Meatballs (page 25), the Soft Pulled Chicken Tacos (page 55), or the Forbidden Rice Cakes with Smoked Salmon and Crispy Capers (page 44). For a sit-down dinner, the Mini Tomato Soups with Crispy Parmesan Tuiles (page 66) are a favorite of mine. The soups have a cute factor and are the perfect appetite teaser to begin your dinner.

Starters are a great opportunity to play and experiment with different serving ideas. Things like mismatched jars, vintage plates, or scarred long pieces of wood are edgier than regular bowls and plates, and make for interesting presentation and conversation. There are no rules here, the only boundary is your imagination, so run with it!

Warm Olives with Grilled Lemons

INGREDIENTS

1 cup Niçoise olives (these
   are the tiny French
   variety)

1 cup kalamata olives

1 cup Italian Bella di
   Cerignola olives

1 cup Picholine olives

1 cup oil-cured olives

⅔ cup extra virgin olive oil

2 sprigs fresh rosemary

2 sprigs fresh thyme

2 sprigs fresh oregano

1 Tbsp chili flakes

2 lemons, quartered and
   grilled (garnish; see note)

MAKES 5 CUPS

Olives are the go-to food for tapas and drinks. This is the perfect side dish, appetizer, or snack to enjoy with pre-dinner cocktails, or pack them into a preserving jar as a host or hostess gift. Mix up the varieties to suit what you like best.

---

1 Place all of the olives in a large colander and spray with water to wash the brine away. Shake well. It is best to do this a few hours ahead to let the olives air-dry.

2 When the olives are dry, warm the oil in a high-sided sauté pan set on low heat. Place the dry olives in the pan with the warm oil and turn the heat off. Toss to coat.

3 With a meat pounder or the back of a cleaver, bash the sprigs of herbs. This will break the leaves and stems and release the fragrant flavors. Add the herb sprigs and the chili flakes to the pan of olives, and warm through. Transfer the whole mixture to a decorative serving bowl, give it a squeeze of lemon juice from the grilled lemons, and garnish the edge with the lemon quarters. Serve warm.

NOTE
To grill the lemons, heat a dry nonstick pan or barbecue to medium heat, place the quartered lemons cut side down, and let them cook until golden, about 5 minutes per side. This process allows the lemons to be succulent and sweet.

Dates Wrapped in Crispy Pancetta

Quick, easy, and more importantly, tasty. I like to use spicy pancetta for that extra kick. You can prepare these perfect little pre-dinner cocktail bites a day ahead and chill; just be sure to remove them an hour before frying so they are not cold in the middle.

---

1 Cut the dates almost in half, taking care not to go through all the way; you want to leave a bit of a hinge. Cut the cheese into 24 cubes, and cut the jalapeño slices in half. Open the dates and stuff each with a cube of the cheese and a slice of jalapeño. Pinch the dates shut and wrap each tightly and entirely with a piece of pancetta. Place the wrapped date in the palm of your hand and squeeze it tight so that everything sticks together.

2 Preheat your oven to 300°F and heat a nonstick fry pan to medium heat. Add the prepared dates to the pan, but do not overcrowd it, as you want these little bites to be crispy. Working in batches if necessary, fry on all sides until they are golden brown, about 5 to 7 minutes. Shake the pan occasionally and turn the dates to ensure browning is uniform.

3 As they finish cooking, transfer to a baking sheet and place in the oven to keep warm. When you are ready to serve, transfer to a serving dish and serve warm.

NOTE

I have suggested half a jalapeño slice, but if you like it hot, go crazy and use the whole slice. If you aren't into heat at all, simply eliminate the jalapeños. I have also called for a few extra slices of pancetta in the event that some slices are small and you need additional bits to cover the dates.

INGREDIENTS

24 soft dried pitted dates

6 oz Comté cheese (fontina or Emmentaler also work well)

12 pickled jalapeño slices, blotted dry on paper towel (see note)

15 thin slices Italian pancetta, halved (see note)

MAKES 24 PIECES

Prosciutto and Pear Wedges with Balsamic Pearls

INGREDIENTS

8 slices Italian prosciutto, trimmed of any fat

2 medium Bartlett pears, cored, halved, and cut into 4 slices per half

8 oz Stilton or Gorgonzola cheese, evenly sliced

1 cup fresh arugula, long stems removed

¼ cup balsamic pearls (garnish; see page 4)

MAKES 16 WEDGES

Simplicity is often the best choice for a starter, especially when combined with fresh ingredients. It does not come any tastier than the combination of juicy, succulent pears with arugula and Stilton cheese, gently cloaked by slices of Italian prosciutto. The sweet highlight is a delightful garnish of balsamic pearls.

---

1 Lay the prosciutto slices on your work surface and cut in half lengthwise. Lay a slice of pear on one end of each piece of prosciutto, then top with a slice of Stilton or Gorgonzola cheese and a few arugula leaves. Roll up, set on a serving plate, and garnish with a few balsamic pearls.

Crispy Chicken Coins

INGREDIENTS

1 lb boneless, skinless
    chicken breasts, minced,
    or 1 lb ground chicken

⅓ cup finely chopped fresh
    cilantro

1 large free-range egg,
    lightly beaten

1 large shallot, finely minced

2 Tbsp snipped fresh chives

1 Tbsp fish sauce

1 tsp chili paste (see page 4)

1 Kaffir lime leaf, spine
    discarded then finely
    minced (see note)

½ cup white sesame seeds

½ cup black sesame seeds

Roasted grapeseed oil, for
    frying

Lime wedges (garnish)

1 cup sweet Thai chili sauce
    or chipotle mayonnaise,
    for dipping

MAKES 24 COINS

Chicken is one of those neutral proteins that kids, adults, and even picky eaters will eat. The challenge is creating something different, both in presentation and taste. I came up with the checkerboard look for a visual twist, and the Thai-influenced flavors for a lively kick.

1 In a large bowl, combine the minced chicken, cilantro, egg, shallot, chives, fish sauce, chili paste, and lime leaf. Mix well to ensure all the flavors are evenly distributed. Measure out 24 heaping tablespoons of the mixture and shape into small coins.

2 Place the white sesame seeds in a small dish and the black sesame seeds in another small dish. Dredge half of the coins in white seeds and half in black seeds to coat all sides. Place the coated coins on a tray and chill for about 30 minutes.

3 Heat a drizzle of grapeseed oil in a nonstick fry pan over medium-high heat. Once the oil is hot, cook the coins for about 2 minutes on each side, or until golden brown and cooked through.

4 Alternating colors, lay the coins on a serving platter to resemble a checkerboard. Serve with lime wedges and sweet Thai chili sauce or chipotle mayonnaise on the side.

NOTES

You can find Kaffir lime leaves at specialty Asian markets, but if they are unavailable, you can substitute 1 teaspoon of lime zest.

Given their great flavor profile, these could also be turned into a main course by making them into burgers. I would match them with crispy Sweet Potato Fries (page 152).

Spicy Asian Glazed Tofu

With diets going in every direction, you need a diverse recipe repertoire to keep all your family and friends happy. This recipe will comfort all the vegetarians in your life. Tofu is a great source of protein and contains eight essential amino acids. I was never a fan of tofu—perhaps it was the preparation—but this is a game changer.

---

1 Drain the liquid from the tofu, pat dry, and let sit for 10 minutes in paper towel to draw out most of the moisture. Cut into 1-inch blocks. Dredge the blocks in the rice flour and shake off the excess. Set aside.

2 To make the sauce, mix the soy sauce, grapeseed oil, sesame oil, ginger, garlic, and chili paste together in a small bowl, then set aside. This mixture can be prepared up to 3 days before serving and kept in the refrigerator.

3 Heat the grapeseed oil in a large nonstick fry pan over medium heat. When the oil is hot, add the flour-dredged blocks of tofu, taking care not to overcrowd them, and leaving enough space between so they crisp and do not steam. Fry in batches, turning the tofu as it fries so each side is evenly browned, about 2 to 3 minutes per side. Remove to a paper-towel-lined plate as the tofu cooks. Once all the tofu is cooked, use a paper towel to mop up the frying oil from the pan. Return all tofu blocks to the pan.

4 With the heat on low, pour in the sauce and toss the pan to ensure all the tofu blocks are well coated. The mixture will immediately thicken and glaze the tofu. Remove from heat right away, transfer the tofu to a serving plate, and pour any excess sauce over top. Serve hot, with toothpicks.

TOFU

1 lb firm or medium-firm tofu (see note)
½ cup rice flour
⅓ cup roasted grapeseed oil, for frying
Fancy toothpicks, for serving

SAUCE

2 Tbsp soy sauce
2 Tbsp roasted grapeseed oil
2 Tbsp toasted sesame oil (see page 5)
1 Tbsp grated ginger (see note, page 94)
2 cloves garlic, minced
2 tsp chili paste (see page 4)

SERVES 6 TO 8

NOTE

Tofu comes in many textures, but for this recipe, use firm or medium-firm. Soft tofu will not crisp up enough.

Sushi Rice Blocks

Sushi is generally the first thing that disappears from any party table. This simple version can help cut the costs of purchasing, and make you look like a star.

INGREDIENTS

1 ½ cups sushi rice

5 Tbsp sushi seasoning (see note)

⅓ cup wasabi mayonnaise or wasabi mustard (see note, page 44)

½ lb sliced sushi-grade tuna, salmon, or other fish, or 18 cooked, shelled prawns, blotted dry and cut in half lengthwise

Green onion, sliced (garnish)

Soy sauce, for dipping

SPECIAL EQUIPMENT

Rectangular silicone mold (see page 8)

MAKES 36 SUSHI BLOCKS

1 Wash the rice several times until the water runs clear. Drain the rice and place in a small pot, add 2 ¼ cups of water, cover, and bring to a boil. Turn down to a simmer and cook until all the water is absorbed, about 20 minutes.

2 Immediately remove the rice from the pot, spread it on a cookie sheet, sprinkle the sushi seasoning evenly over top, and let cool.

3 Once the steam subsides, press the rice into the cavities in the silicone mold. Chill in the fridge for 30 minutes, then remove from the mold. To assemble, smear a bit of wasabi mayo or mustard on top of each rice cube and top with a slice of green onion and your choice of seafood. Chill until ready to serve. Serve with soy sauce on the side.

NOTES

You can layer a piece of nori (seaweed) in the center of the rice when pressing the rice into the mold to make your homemade sushi a bit more authentic.

Do not confuse sushi seasoning with rice vinegar. Rice vinegar is made by fermenting the sugars present in rice into alcohol, then further fermenting the alcohol into vinegar. Sushi seasoning, or seasoned rice vinegar, is simply rice vinegar with added sugar and salt. It takes the guesswork out of seasoning the sushi rice.

Really Good Meatballs

Meatballs used to be rather ho-hum in my mind, just something to tide you over when visiting giant furniture stores. My mixture of veal, pork, and beef truly takes them to the next level. Pine nuts and grated Parmesan elevate them that much more. Who needs the spaghetti? These can either be pan-fried or baked; whichever you prefer.

---

1 If baking the meatballs, preheat your oven to 375°F.

2 Soak the bread in a shallow bowl of water for about 20 minutes. Squeeze it dry and chop it fine. Discard the water.

3 While the bread is soaking, place the garlic, shallots, beaten eggs, and mustard in a large bowl. Add the meats, Worcestershire, chili paste, ½ cup of the Parmesan, the basil, parsley, pine nuts, and chopped soaked bread. Mix well, ensuring all ingredients are well combined. Using a portion scoop or soupspoon, roll the mixture into balls. Size is personal.

4 In a large sauté pan over medium-high heat, panfry the meatballs until well browned on all sides, about 10 to 15 minutes, depending on size. (If baking, place on a parchment-lined cookie sheet and bake for 30 to 40 minutes, or until browned, turning halfway through to ensure even browning.)

5 In the same pan, heat the sauce until simmering; stir in a splash of vodka for that optional extra kick. Ladle the sauce into an ovenproof serving dish, place the browned meatballs on top, garnish with remaining Parmesan, and put under the broiler until the cheese bubbles, about 1 minute. This pairs perfectly with rustic country bread for dipping and sopping. Spaghetti is optional.

INGREDIENTS

4 slices white bread
4 cloves garlic, minced
2 large shallots, finely minced
2 large free-range eggs, lightly beaten
2 heaping Tbsp Dijon mustard
¾ lb ground pork
¾ lb ground veal
¾ lb lean ground beef
2 Tbsp Worcestershire sauce
2 Tbsp chili paste (see page 4)
1⅓ cups freshly grated Parmesan cheese
½ cup chopped fresh basil
½ cup chopped fresh Italian parsley
½ cup pine nuts
1 jar (12 oz) good-quality tomato sauce (I like Lidia's Tomato Basil Sauce or Rao's Vodka Sauce)
Splash of vodka (optional)

MAKES 50 MEDIUM-SIZED MEATBALLS

Seeded Baguette with Shaved Beef and Béarnaise

Beef is always a popular item at any cocktail party. The challenge is finding an interesting cracker or bread to mound the beef on. Solution: a seeded baguette! The seeded bread is a great base for your beef, so start shaving! (The beef, that is.)

---

1 Preheat your oven to 350°F.

2 Mix all of the seeds and the garlic together in a bowl. Slice the bread into ¼-inch slices, and brush with the ⅓ cup of olive oil, spreading evenly to the edges. Don't be lazy and dab just the middle; your effort to meet the crusts will be worth it. Press the seeds into the bread so they adhere, then shake off the excess and continue with the remaining slices.

3 Place the seeded bread on a cookie sheet and bake for 15 minutes, or until the bread slices are crisp and cracker-like. Remove and let cool. These will keep for 1 week in an airtight container.

4 To prepare the beef, rub the 2 tablespoons of olive oil into your hands and massage the beef, ensuring the oil coats it well. Shake the salt and pepper rub onto a plate, then roll the tenderloin in the rub, ensuring it is well coated on all sides.

5 If cooking in the oven, increase the heat to 425°F. Transfer the beef to a grill pan, and sear on high heat to brown all sides, then place in the oven to finish. If barbecuing, sear the meat on high, then turn down to medium heat. Cook until the internal temperature reaches 140°F, about 15 to 20 minutes for a medium-rare finish. The timing will vary depending on your barbecue or oven, so check often with a meat thermometer. Let the beef rest at least 15 minutes before slicing. Shave finely, then set aside.

6 To serve, lay the seeded toasts on your serving plate. Top toasts with shaved beef, and finish with dollops of onion jam and béarnaise.

SEEDED BAGUETTE

¼ cup chia seeds

¼ cup sunflower seeds

¼ cup black sesame seeds

¼ cup white sesame seeds

¼ cup flax seeds

2 tsp granulated garlic or garlic powder

1 day-old baguette (I prefer to use a ficelle)

⅓ cup extra virgin olive oil

BEEF

2 Tbsp extra virgin olive oil

1 ½ lb beef tenderloin, trimmed of all fat

½ cup salt and pepper rub (I like Côte d'Azur Salt & Pepper Rub), or ¼ cup kosher salt plus ¼ cup coarse cracked black pepper

1 cup Fig, Garlic, and Onion Jam (page 169; or use store-bought)

1 jar (4 oz) béarnaise sauce

MAKES 24 TO 30 PIECES

Aged Balderson Cheddar and Paprika Crisps

INGREDIENTS

6 Tbsp unsalted butter,
    room temperature

1 cup unbleached all-
    purpose flour

2 tsp sweet smoked Spanish
    paprika (see page 5)

2 cups grated aged
    Balderson cheddar
    (see note)

Fleur de sel, for topping

MAKES 60 CRISPS

Who doesn't love a crisp little cheese coin that bursts with flavor and pairs perfectly with wine? The addition of smoked Spanish paprika gives an edge to what would otherwise just be a cheese cracker. These can double-duty as a host or hostess gift. You can also make them ahead and freeze unbaked. When the occasion calls for crisps, simply slice and bake without a mess.

---

1 Place the butter in a medium bowl and, using an electric mixer, beat until light and creamy, about 5 minutes. Add the flour and paprika and continue to mix until combined. Add the cheese and continue to mix until smooth and evenly incorporated throughout.

2 Turn the mixture onto a lightly floured board and knead until it forms a cohesive and smooth dough, about 10 minutes.

3 Divide into four equal pieces and roll into 1-inch-diameter logs. Wrap in plastic wrap, squeeze the ends tight to ensure you have even logs, and chill for 1 hour. At this point, these can be frozen for up to 2 months, if desired.

4 When you are ready to bake the crisps, preheat your oven to 400°F.

5 Slice the chilled logs into ¼-inch disks, and place them on a cookie sheet lined with parchment paper or a nonstick baking mat. Top each with a pinch of fleur de sel, and bake in the oven for 7 to 10 minutes. You want them cooked through but not browned. Remove and place on a wire rack to cool. The crisps will keep for 3 to 5 days in an airtight container, and can be frozen for up to 1 month.

NOTE

If you can't find Balderson cheddar, you can use any other variety of aged cheddar.

Pita Chips

Homemade pita chips are the easiest crisp to make. You can mix things up by using different seasonings, but if plain is your game, sea salt and good olive oil are all you need.

———————————

1 Preheat your oven to 350°F.

2 Lay the pita rounds on your work surface. Insert the tip of a small paring knife into the side seam of a pita. Once the knife is inserted, it is easy to cut the round in half, giving you two pita circles. Repeat with the remaining pitas.

3 Lightly brush each side of the pita circles with oil, then sprinkle one side with the spice blend. Be cautious with the spice blend, as you do not want that flavor to dominate. Cut each circle into six wedges and lay them spice side up on a cookie sheet. Do not stack on top of each other, as you want them crispy on both sides.

4 Bake for about 12 to 15 minutes, or until crispy and light golden brown. The chips will keep for 1 week in a sealed container.

NOTE
Dukkah hails from the Middle East and is a blend of hazelnuts, sesame seeds, cumin, coriander, flaked sea salt, and ground black pepper. It is perfect for rubs and spice coatings.

INGREDIENTS
Six 6-inch pita rounds
⅔ cup extra virgin olive oil
½ cup dukkah (see note), za'atar (see recipe introduction, page 32), or your favorite spice blend

MAKES 72 CHIPS

Charred Eggplant and Za'atar Dip

INGREDIENTS

1 whole head garlic

1 tsp extra virgin olive oil

1 medium eggplant (about 1 lb)

¼ cup mascarpone cheese
   (see note, page 162)

2 Tbsp tahini paste

1 tsp fresh lemon zest

1 tsp fresh lemon juice

1 tsp za'atar, plus extra for
   garnish

2 tsp kosher salt

Freshly ground pepper

Julienned lemon zest
   (optional garnish)

MAKES 1 HEAPING CUP

Photo on page 10

Dips of various flavors are always a welcome "help yourself" invitation on any table. Eggplant is widely available, and with a bit of seasoning and blackening, this dip can really start a party! Charring the eggplant deepens its otherwise rather ho-hum flavor, while za'atar, the Middle Eastern spice blend of sesame seeds, dried thyme, and sumac, adds a touch of the exotic.

---

1 Preheat your oven to 325°F.

2 Cut the top ¼ inch off the garlic head, rub with the oil, and wrap in foil. Bake for about 45 to 60 minutes or until the garlic is soft and light golden brown. Cool, peel off the papery skin, and set the roasted cloves aside.

3 Increase the oven heat to 375°F. Cut the eggplant in half lengthwise. Place both halves cut side down on an open gas flame or barbecue until the surfaces char all over, about 10 minutes. Once the surfaces are charred, transfer to a baking sheet cut side up and roast for a further 20 minutes, or until the eggplant is soft. Remove and set aside until cool enough to handle.

4 Peel back the skin from the eggplant and transfer the pulp to the bowl of a food processor. Add the roasted garlic cloves, mascarpone, tahini, lemon zest and juice, and za'atar. Process the mixture until it is smooth and creamy. Add the kosher salt and ground pepper; taste for seasoning and adjust as required. Garnish with a sprinkle of za'atar and julienned lemon zest, if using.

5 This dip can be made up to 3 days ahead and kept in the refrigerator. Serve with Pita Chips (page 31).

Spicy Hummus with Crispy Chickpeas

This dip is a global classic, with versions that abound. The standard ingredients include garlic, tahini, lemon juice, cumin, and olive oil. Twists on classics are always a good thing, so I chose to add Moroccan spice, and top with crispy whole chickpeas, a crumble of feta, torn cilantro, and pomegranate seeds.

---

1 To make the hummus, place the drained chickpeas in the bowl of a food processor. Add the lemon juice, tahini, and garlic, and purée until smooth. Scrape down the sides of the bowl, sprinkle in the Moroccan spice, cumin, sea salt, and pepper to taste, and pulse until combined.

2 With the machine running, slowly drizzle in the olive oil. Taste for seasoning and adjust if needed. If the hummus seems too thick for your preference, add a few tablespoons of the reserved chickpea liquid and pulse. Transfer the hummus to a rectangular serving dish.

3 To make the crispy chickpeas, lay 1 cup of chickpeas on paper towel for about 20 minutes to remove most of the moisture. Place the rice flour in a bowl, add the dry chickpeas, and toss to ensure they are evenly coated. Place the chickpeas in a mesh sieve and give them a shake or two to remove any excess flour. Heat the oil in a pan over medium-high heat until it sizzles when you drop in a chickpea. In small batches, about a handful at a time to avoid overcrowding, fry the chickpeas until crisp, about 2 to 3 minutes. Remove with a slotted spoon onto a plate lined with paper towel and let cool.

4 Sprinkle the chickpeas over the hummus, along with the feta, cilantro, and pomegranate seeds, if using, and a drizzle of olive oil.

5 Serve with Seeded Baguette (page 27) or Pita Chips (page 31). The hummus can be made up to 5 days ahead and kept in the refrigerator, while the crispy chickpeas can be kept in an airtight container for up to 2 days—if they last that long!

HUMMUS

1 can (19 oz) chickpeas, drained, liquid reserved
4 Tbsp fresh lemon juice
3 Tbsp tahini paste
2 cloves garlic
2 tsp Moroccan seasoning spice blend
¼ tsp ground cumin
Pinch of sea salt
Freshly ground pepper
½ cup extra virgin olive oil, plus more to finish
1 cup feta cheese, crumbled (optional)
½ cup torn fresh cilantro leaves (optional)
½ cup pomegranate seeds (optional)

CRISPY CHICKPEAS

1 cup drained and rinsed canned chickpeas
½ cup rice flour
1 cup roasted grapeseed oil, for frying

MAKES 3 CUPS OF HUMMUS AND 1 CUP OF CRISPY CHICKPEAS

Photo on page 10

Artichoke, Parmesan, and Cannellini Bean Dip

INGREDIENTS

1 whole head garlic

1 tsp plus 2 Tbsp extra virgin olive oil

1 large shallot, finely minced

1 can (14 oz) water-packed artichoke hearts, drained

1 tsp fresh thyme leaves

1 tsp chili paste, plus extra for garnish (optional; see page 4)

1 can (14 oz) Italian cannellini beans, drained and rinsed

1 package (5.2 oz) Boursin cheese, original flavor

⅓ cup freshly grated Parmesan cheese

1 tsp fresh lemon zest

Sea salt and freshly ground pepper

MAKES 3 CUPS

Photo on page 10

Several years ago, my dear friend and television broadcaster Fanny Kiefer invited me on her talk show. She was promoting a respected citywide competition called Canstruction, for the purpose of increasing contributions to the Vancouver Food Bank. My challenge was to create something tasty from a can. Canned products are generally not the primary go-to for chefs, but my challenge turned into a delicious recipe for a simple homemade dip.

————————

1 Preheat your oven to 325°F.

2 Cut about ¼ inch off the top of the garlic head. Drizzle with 1 teaspoon of olive oil. Wrap in foil and close loosely. Bake for about 45 to 60 minutes or until the garlic is soft and light golden brown. Cool, remove the cloves from the papery skin, and set aside.

3 Heat a fry pan to medium heat, then add 2 tablespoons of olive oil and the shallot. Slowly sauté the shallot for 2 to 3 minutes, taking care not to brown.

4 While the shallot is cooking, cut the artichokes into pieces and add to the fry pan, tossing to combine. Add the thyme and the chili paste, if using. Turn the heat to low and let the artichokes drink in the flavor for 6 to 8 minutes.

5 Meanwhile, pour the drained beans into the bowl of a food processor, along with the peeled, roasted garlic, Boursin cheese, Parmesan, and lemon zest. Pulse a few times, then add the artichoke mixture and purée until smooth and creamy. Taste for seasoning and adjust with sea salt and freshly ground pepper. Garnish with chili paste if you like an extra kick.

6 Serve with assorted crackers (see Seeded Baguette on page 27, or Pita Chips on page 31) and wine, of course! This dip can be made up to 5 days ahead and kept in the refrigerator.

Truffle Parmesan Popcorn

OMG, this is such a treat! If you like popcorn, this will be a love affair, because it takes popcorn to a totally different level; perhaps you could even sell it! This starter goes well with cocktails or wine, and it may become addictive.

INGREDIENTS

18 cups freshly popped popcorn (start with 1 cup popcorn kernels)

2 tsp truffle salt (use more if you are a truffle addict)

⅔ cup melted unsalted butter

1 cup fresh finely grated Parmesan cheese

MAKES 18 CUPS

1 Place the popped popcorn in a large rectangular roasting pan or any bowl that will allow you to mix the popcorn easily. Sprinkle over the truffle salt, then the melted butter, and finally the Parmesan. Use your hands to mix and distribute the flavors evenly.

2 Transfer to cute popcorn boxes and wait for the movie to start.

Truffle Pizza

In an attempt to make entertaining simple and delicious, I created this great pizza to serve as an appetizer with drinks. Effort required: little. Accolades: many. Make lots; they disappear fast!

---

1 Preheat your oven to 450°F.

2 Lay the pizza crusts on your counter and spread the mascarpone cheese evenly to the edges. Top with a thin layer of the truffle spread, about 2 to 3 tablespoons per pizza. Finish with a light sprinkle of Parmesan. At this point you can make as many as needed; simply place a sheet of parchment between each pizza and stack them to save counter space. They can also be placed in a freezer bag this way and frozen for 4 to 6 weeks.

3 When ready to bake, transfer to two rimless cookie sheets. Bake for 5 to 8 minutes (or see note). Watch carefully, as they cook quickly. To get a super-crisp pizza-oven crust, slide the pizzas off the cookie sheet and let them rest directly on the oven rack for the last minute of baking. Remove, cut into wedges, and serve immediately.

INGREDIENTS

Four 8-inch thin pre-made
   pizza crusts (see note)
2 cups mascarpone cheese
   (see note, page 162)
1 jar (5.6 oz) black truffle
   spread (I like La Madia
   La Tartufata Black Truffle
   Spread & Topping)
1 cup freshly grated
   Parmesan cheese

**EACH PIZZA SERVES 2 TO
4 AS AN APPETIZER**

NOTES

Choose pizza crusts from the freezer section of a good gourmet store. They are generally made with "oo" flour and are nice and thin.

In the summer, I use my barbecue to cook the pizzas. The crust is perfect and it brings the party outdoors in a hurry. They cook very fast, about 2 to 3 minutes with the lid down on medium-low, as all you are doing is melting the cheese and crisping the crust.

Flatbread Rolls with Crab and Arugula

INGREDIENTS

1 ½ lb fresh Dungeness crab
    meat

½ lime, for squeezing

3 flatbreads, thin and
    charred (at least 8 inches
    square)

2 cups fresh arugula, long
    stems removed

1 cup chipotle mayonnaise
    or sweet Thai chili sauce,
    for dipping

TROPICAL GUACAMOLE

2 ripe avocados, coarsely
    chopped

½ ripe papaya, peeled,
    seeded, and diced

1 large shallot, finely minced

1 large clove garlic, minced

1 cup grape tomatoes,
    quartered

2 Tbsp Worcestershire sauce

1 Tbsp fresh lime juice

1 to 2 tsp your favorite hot
    sauce

½ cup chopped fresh
    cilantro

Fleur de sel and freshly
    ground pepper

**MAKES 6 STARTER-SIZE
ROLLS OR 24 BITE-SIZE
APPETIZERS**

There is a huge array of flatbreads on the market now, so choose the one you like best, ensuring that it is fairly thin and has char marks, which indicate it has been wood-fired. This can be served as a nice light appetizer but also makes a great first course.

---

1 Blot the crab on paper towel, taking care to remove any pieces of shell. Break apart the large pieces. Give it a squeeze of fresh lime juice and chill until assembly.

2 To make the tropical guacamole, place the avocados, papaya, shallot, and garlic in a medium bowl. Using a large fork, mash the ingredients together, but do not mush; you want chunks about the size of your thumbnail. Add the tomatoes, Worcestershire sauce, lime juice, and hot sauce (using an amount to your taste). Stir to combine. Add the cilantro, taste for seasoning, and adjust as required with fleur de sel and pepper.

3 To assemble, lay one piece of flatbread on your work surface and cut it into an 8-inch square. Spread a layer of guacamole lightly over the flatbread square, then spread over a third of the crab, sprinkle on a third of the arugula, and roll up. Repeat with remaining flatbreads to create two more rolls. You can either cut each roll in half on the diagonal to serve as a starter (see note), or into 1-inch pieces for appetizer bites. Serve with chipotle mayonnaise or sweet chili sauce.

NOTE

If you choose to serve as a starter, dress the plate with another small handful of arugula, and enhance with a squeeze of fresh lime and fleur de sel. Put the dipping sauce in a small condiment cup.

Susie's Chorizo Quesadillas with Cilantro Cream

QUESADILLAS
4 oz soft-style chorizo (hot or mild) (see note)
Eight 8-inch flour tortillas
1 cup grated Monterey Jack cheese

CILANTRO CREAM
1 cup tightly packed fresh cilantro, leaves and stems
¾ cup sour cream
¾ cup plain cream cheese, room temperature
2 small jalapeño peppers, halved, seeded, and coarsely chopped
1 green onion, finely chopped
Pinch of kosher salt

MAKES 24 WEDGES AND 2 CUPS OF CILANTRO CREAM

My dear friend Susan Meister is the owner of Fabulous Foods Catering in Vancouver. One of the most requested appetizers on her list are these chorizo quesadillas. Just so you know, one is never enough. Thank you, Susie!

1 Cut the casings from the chorizo and place the meat in a fry pan on medium-high heat. Using a fork, break up the chorizo until it resembles ground meat. Continue frying on medium-high heat until the chorizo is crispy. Transfer to a paper-towel-lined plate to absorb any excess oil.

2 Lay four of the tortillas on your work surface. Spread 1 ½ tablespoons of the cooked chorizo on each one. Evenly sprinkle with ¼ cup of the grated Monterey Jack cheese, then sandwich with the remaining tortillas, pressing down with your hands to seal the edges. Once they are all prepared and cooled, they can be stacked and stored in a resealable bag; make sure you push all the air out before you seal the bag. These can be made 3 days ahead of time and kept refrigerated until serving time.

3 To make the cilantro cream, place the cilantro, sour cream, cream cheese, chopped jalapeños, chopped green onion, and salt into the bowl of a food processor. Pulse a few times, then run the machine until the mixture is smooth and creamy. Scrape the bowl down and ensure the entire mixture is smooth. Taste for seasoning and adjust with salt if needed.

4 When you're ready to serve, heat a nonstick fry pan over medium heat, slide in a prepared quesadilla, and cook until golden brown on both sides, about 2 to 3 minutes per side, or until you can see the cheese oozing and melted. Repeat with the remaining quesadillas. Place the cooked quesadillas onto a cutting board and slice each into six wedges. Transfer to a serving plate accompanied by a bowl of the cilantro cream. Serve warm.

NOTE
Soft chorizo is like a regular sausage in a casing that requires cooking; not to be confused with the hard, cured type of chorizo that can be eaten like salami.

Coyote Corn Cakes with Seared Scallops

INGREDIENTS

Kosher salt

3 medium russet potatoes, peeled and chopped

1 can (12 oz) corn kernels, drained and rinsed

2 large shallots, finely minced

¼ cup finely snipped fresh chives

1 large free-range egg, lightly beaten

2 Tbsp mayonnaise (I like Hellmann's)

1 heaping Tbsp Dijon mustard

2 tsp ground cumin

This relatively easy corn cake serves as a crispy holder for the seared scallops. Make sure you use corn kernels and not creamed corn! You can switch out the scallops for spot prawns or salmon if you like.

---

1 Bring a large pot of water to boil, add some kosher salt, and drop in the potatoes. Cook the potatoes until a knife easily pierces through them, about 15 to 20 minutes. Drain the boiled potatoes, then return them to the pot with the heat on low to dry them out for just a few minutes. Remove the potatoes from the pot, mash them well, and set aside.

2 Heat a cast iron or fry pan on medium-high heat. Add the corn and dry-roast until the kernels are browned and dry, about 10 minutes. Keep shaking the pan periodically to promote even browning. Set aside.

3 In a large bowl, mix together the mashed potatoes, roasted corn, shallots, chives, egg, mayonnaise, mustard, cumin, lime zest, piri piri sauce to taste, oregano, and salt to taste. Mix well to distribute all the ingredients evenly. Form into 1 ½-inch cakes and place on a parchment-lined cookie sheet until ready to cook. The cakes can be made up to a day ahead and kept chilled until ready to fry.

4 In a small bowl, mix together the scallops, ⅓ cup oil, salt, and garlic. Set aside.

5 Heat a nonstick fry pan on medium-high heat, add just enough olive oil to lightly coat the pan, and fry the prepared corn cakes until browned on both sides. This should take about 3 minutes for each side. Transfer to a serving dish as they cook. Do not overcrowd the pan; fry the cakes in batches, or use two pans. The cakes can be fried a few hours before serving and reheated in a 375°F oven for about 10 minutes.

6 When you are ready to serve, heat a nonstick fry pan on medium-high heat. Sear the scallops on both sides until golden, about 1 minute per side; do not overcook. Lay the cooked scallops on top of the warm corn cakes and top with a few chili threads. Serve warm.

2 tsp fresh lime zest

1 to 2 tsp piri piri sauce, or your favorite hot sauce

1 tsp dried oregano

Sea salt

½ lb fresh bay scallops

⅓ cup extra virgin olive oil, plus extra for frying

2 tsp kosher salt

1 large clove garlic, minced

Chili threads (garnish; see note, page 48)

MAKES 20 CORN CAKES

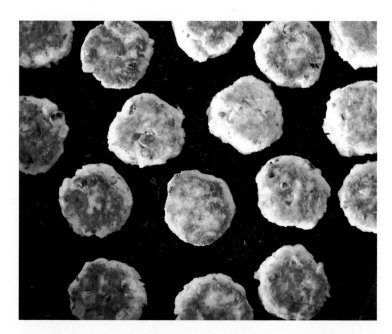

Forbidden Rice Cakes with Smoked Salmon and Crispy Capers

INGREDIENTS

1 cup forbidden rice

1 large free-range egg,
    lightly beaten

2 Tbsp wasabi mustard (see
    note)

2 Tbsp unbleached all-
    purpose flour

1 Tbsp soy sauce

Roasted grapeseed oil, for
    frying

1 cup Crème Fraîche
    (page 169; or use
    store-bought)

8 oz smoked salmon

⅓ cup Crispy Capers
    (garnish; page 168)

Fresh cilantro leaves
    (garnish)

**MAKES 24 TO 30 RICE
CAKES**

Back in the days of imperial China, only the royal house was entitled to eat this special rice—hence the name "forbidden." Thankfully, times have changed and everyone can now enjoy it. The integrity of the rice lies in the intense color, which does not pale when cooked.

———

1 Place the rice and 2 cups of water in a stainless-steel pot, cover, and bring to a boil. Turn down to a simmer and cook until the rice is done and all the water is absorbed, about 15 to 18 minutes. Remove the lid and cool.

2 Beat the egg, wasabi mustard, flour, and soy sauce together, pour over the rice, and mix to combine. Form 2-inch round cakes each about ½ inch thick, making sure they are all evenly sized. Lay them on a cookie sheet. These can be done several hours in advance, covered and stored in the refrigerator, and fried when you are ready to serve.

3 Heat a large nonstick fry pan on medium heat. Add just enough grapeseed oil to glisten the pan. When the oil is hot, begin frying the rice cakes, about 1 minute on each side, or until crisp. Fry in batches and do not overcrowd the pan while frying.

4 As they finish cooking, transfer to a serving platter to cool. Apply a good spread of crème fraîche to the top of each cake. Crown with the smoked salmon and finish with the capers and cilantro.

NOTE

Wasabi mustard is a wasabi-flavored condiment, not to be confused with the wasabi served at sushi restaurants. It can be purchased at Japanese and gourmet stores.

Tina's Tuna Tataki on Sesame Wonton Crisps

WONTON CRISPS

1 package (7.7 oz) 3-inch
    square wonton wrappers

⅓ cup roasted grapeseed
    oil, for brushing

½ cup sesame seeds

TUNA TATAKI

1 lb sushi-grade tuna

1 large shallot, finely minced

3 Tbsp grated ginger (see
    note, page 94)

1 Tbsp toasted sesame oil
    (see page 5)

1 Tbsp soy sauce

1 Tbsp chili paste (see page 4)

1 large clove garlic, minced

1 tsp fresh lime zest

2 tsp fresh lime juice

1 avocado, diced into ¼-inch
    cubes

½ cup tobiko (garnish; see
    note)

Green onion, sliced
    (garnish)

**MAKES 24 TO 30 WONTON
CRISPS**

My daughter Christina's favorite protein is tuna. She could eat it every day, or so she says. This is a take on her recipe, with a few add-ins of my own. While it's easy to make, it is important that the tuna is very fresh and kept chilled until serving time.

---

1 Preheat your oven to 325°F.

2 Lay the wonton wrappers on your work surface, about five at a time. Cut diagonally in half. Lightly brush with the grapeseed oil just enough to glisten, taking care not to drown them in oil. Sprinkle each wrapper with ½ teaspoon of sesame seeds. Repeat with the remaining wonton wrappers. Transfer to a cookie sheet and bake for about 8 to 10 minutes, or until golden brown. Remove from the oven and cool, then transfer to an airtight container until ready to use. You can make these up to 5 days in advance.

3 Dice the tuna into roughly ¼-inch cubes, being careful not to mince it, and then transfer to a bowl and refrigerate. In a separate bowl, mix together the shallot, ginger, sesame oil, soy sauce, chili paste, garlic, and lime zest and juice. Mix well to combine the flavors, then pour the sauce over the chilled tuna and gently mix through. Add the avocado carefully; do not stir vigorously, as you do not want to mush the avocado or bruise the tuna.

4 To serve, place the wonton crisps on a platter and spoon about a tablespoon of the tuna mixture on top. Top each with about ½ teaspoon of tobiko and a few green onion slices.

NOTE
Tobiko is another name for flying fish roe. It is easily available at Japanese stores. The texture has a curious crunch, and the natural color is pinky-orange.

NOTE
Chili threads are very thin, almost wisp-like strands of chili. They are used for garnish and are available online and in some gourmet stores, but don't worry if you can't find them.

Blue Corn Madeleines with Hand-Peeled Shrimp

Madeleine sponge cakes hail from an 18th-century pastry chef named—you guessed it—Madeleine. The cake is distinguished by the shell-shaped pan it is baked in. I have transformed the original sweet version into a savory base for limitless topping options!

———————

1 Preheat your oven to 400°F. Grease the madeleine pans and set aside.

2 In a medium bowl, combine the cornmeal, flour, sugar, baking powder, salt, and paprika. Set aside.

3 In a small bowl, whisk the buttermilk, egg, and melted butter together. Pour this liquid mixture over the bowl of dry ingredients, add 2 tablespoons of the snipped chives, and stir well.

4 Spoon 2 teaspoons of the batter into each cavity of the prepared pans. Tap the filled pans on the counter lightly. This will allow the batter to release any trapped air bubbles and produce evenly baked madeleines without holes. Bake for 6 to 8 minutes or until golden brown. Remove from the oven and allow to cool for no more than 5 minutes, or else they will stick to the pan. Turn the pan over so the madeleines fall out. Set aside until serving time.

5 Blot the shrimp on paper towel to absorb any excess moisture, then place in a small bowl and add the parsley, lemon juice, and fleur de sel and pepper to taste. Mix to combine. Taste for seasoning and adjust as required.

6 To assemble, arrange the baked madeleines on a serving plate. Top each one with a dollop of sour cream, then a small portion of the shrimp mixture. Finish with the remaining chives and chili threads on top.

INGREDIENTS

⅓ cup blue cornmeal
6 Tbsp unbleached all-purpose flour
1 Tbsp sugar
2 tsp baking powder
½ tsp kosher salt
Pinch of sweet smoked Spanish paprika (see page 5)
1 cup buttermilk
1 large free-range egg, lightly beaten
3 Tbsp melted unsalted butter
4 Tbsp snipped fresh chives
½ lb fresh hand-peeled cooked shrimp
¼ cup finely chopped fresh parsley
2 Tbsp fresh lemon juice
Fleur de sel and freshly ground pepper
½ cup sour cream
Chili threads, halved (garnish; see note)

SPECIAL EQUIPMENT

Two 4-inch madeleine pans; the nonstick variety is best

MAKES 24 MADELEINES

Foie Gras Mousse on Toasted Brioche

INGREDIENTS

1 brioche sandwich loaf (see note)

6 oz foie gras mousse, room temperature (see note)

2 Tbsp unsalted butter, room temperature

1 cup cranberry confit (I like Chef Ann Kirseböm's Cranberry & Onion Confit; see note)

Toasted slivered pistachio nuts (garnish; see page 166)

SPECIAL EQUIPMENT

14-inch piping bag

Large star tip

2-inch round fluted cookie cutter

MAKES 24 PIECES

Foie gras is the empress of the culinary world, with a taste like no other. Be it goose or duck, the flavor is sublime! Don't be alarmed about animal cruelty. The ducks in North America are not force-fed; they are a strain that insatiably eat non-stop, consequently enlarging their own livers.

---

1 Slice the brioche into ¼-inch slices. Using your cookie cutter, cut out 24 circles and toast the brioche on both sides in a toaster oven. Or place on a cookie sheet under the broiler for 2 minutes until golden brown. Do not overtoast.

2 Place the foie gras and butter in a medium bowl. With an electric mixer, whip until light and fluffy, about 6 to 8 minutes. Transfer the mixture to a piping bag fitted with a large star tip.

3 Spread ½ teaspoon of cranberry confit onto the toasted brioche circles, then pipe fois gras rosettes on top. Chill until serving time. To serve, transfer to a serving dish and garnish each with toasted pistachio nuts.

NOTES

Foie gras can be purchased at good gourmet stores everywhere. Make certain you purchase the chilled mousse version, not the raw livers.

If brioche bread is not available at your local bakery, simply substitute with sliced white bread. Do not use the crusts.

Chef Ann Kirseböm is a local Vancouver manufacturer and creator of marinades, dressings, and chocolates. Her Cranberry & Onion Confit is a specialty. You can also use the Fig, Garlic, and Onion Jam on page 169.

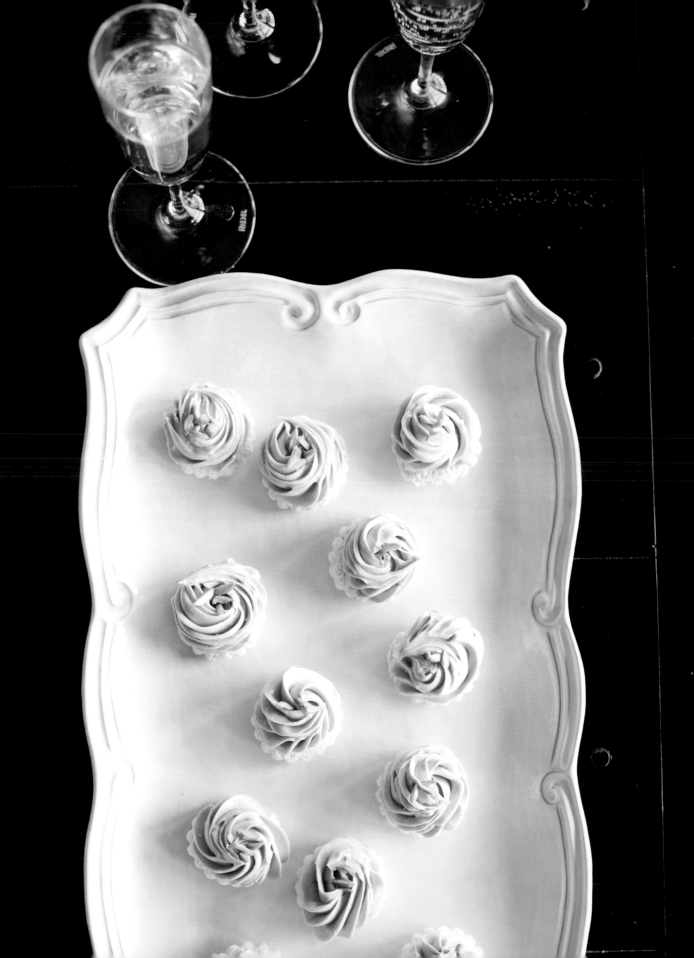

Crispy Corn Tortillas with Shredded Duck

INGREDIENTS

Twelve 6-inch corn tortillas

3 Tbsp roasted grapeseed
oil, for frying

½ barbecued duck (see
recipe introduction)

⅓ cup hoisin sauce

¼ cup chutney (I prefer
mango)

1 cup grated Monterey Jack
or fontina cheese

½ cup chopped dried
cranberries

½ cup chopped toasted
pecans (see page 166)

1 bunch fresh cilantro,
leaves only

SPECIAL EQUIPMENT

2- or 3-inch round cookie
cutter

**MAKES 24 MINI
TORTILLAS**

The easiest, cheapest, and quickest way to execute this recipe is to run to your local Chinese takeout and purchase half of a barbecued duck. Ask them to cut the duck in half, *not* in pieces; this makes it easy to pull the meat from the bones. With the hard part taken care of, simply assemble the tortillas and enjoy the praise.

---

1 Preheat your oven to 375°F.

2 Lay the tortillas on your work surface. Using your cookie cutter, punch out 24 circles. Heat the oil over medium heat in a shallow nonstick fry pan and, working in batches, crisp the circles on both sides, about 1 minute per side. Remove and transfer to paper towels to absorb any excess oil. Set aside. These can be done up to 1 day in advance and stored in an airtight container.

3 Remove all the meat from the duck, and discard the bones and skin. Shred the meat with two forks or your hands, and place it in a large bowl. Drizzle the hoisin and chutney over the duck, add the cheese and cranberries, and lightly toss to distribute the ingredients evenly. Set aside until serving time. This can be made ahead of time and refrigerated until you are ready to serve, up to 2 days in advance.

4 To serve, preheat your oven to 375°F (if necessary). Lay the tortilla circles on a cookie sheet, place a heaping tablespoon of the duck mixture on the circles, and bake for 5 to 6 minutes, or until the cheese melts. Remove from the oven, top each with a sprinkle of toasted pecans, and finish with a cilantro leaf.

Soft Pulled Chicken Tacos

Who doesn't love tacos? One way to dress these up a bit is to use cute clothespins to hold them shut, as in the photo. Tacos made easy and tasty. What more do you want?

---

1 Preheat your oven to 375°F.

2 Rub the chicken thighs with the dry rub and transfer to a small roasting pan that will fit the thighs in a snug fashion. Pour the jar of salsa over top and cover with foil. Bake in the oven for 1 hour, or until the meat easily falls apart when a fork is inserted into the thighs. If there is an excessive amount of liquid, pour it off. Remove the foil and bake for a further 15 minutes.

3 While the chicken is cooking, warm the oil in a fry pan over medium heat. Sauté the onion and garlic until the onion has softened but is not brown, about 10 minutes. Turn off the heat, transfer to a bowl, and add the black beans, corn salsa, and cilantro.

4 Adjust the oven to 300°F. Wrap the tortillas in foil and place in the oven to warm through, about 10 to 15 minutes. Shred the chicken and place in a serving bowl. To serve, spoon the shredded chicken on the warmed tortillas, followed by the bean and corn mixture, the shredded lettuce, a slice of avocado, and a dollop of sour cream, if using.

INGREDIENTS

6 boneless, skinless chicken thighs
½ cup your favorite dry spice rub (NOMU has a great range of rubs)
1 jar (16 oz) your favorite salsa
2 Tbsp roasted grapeseed oil
½ cup finely diced sweet onion
1 clove garlic, minced
2 cups cooked or canned black beans, drained and rinsed
1 cup corn salsa
½ cup coarsely chopped fresh cilantro
Eight 6-inch flour tortillas
1 cup shredded iceberg lettuce
1 avocado, sliced
Sour cream (optional garnish)

SERVES 8

Mini Halloumi Sliders

INGREDIENTS

50 grape tomatoes (about 1 lb)

Balsamic vinegar, for
    drizzling

2 cloves garlic, finely minced

Sea salt

1 lb halloumi cheese (see
    note)

¼ cup unbleached all-
    purpose flour

1 tsp roasted grapeseed oil

24 mini burger buns

1 cup Fig, Garlic, and Onion
    Jam (page 169; or use
    store-bought)

½ cup chipotle mayonnaise

1 heaping cup baby lettuce
    leaves

1 small jar (6 oz) French
    cornichon pickles,
    drained

Fancy skewers

**MAKES 24 CUTE LITTLE
SLIDERS**

I created this cute little burger for a charity event. I wanted to serve an innovative veggie appetizer, and this was the outcome. Carnivores and vegetarians alike gave it two thumbs up! I urge you to make these burgers, big or small.

---

1 Preheat your oven to 250°F.

2 Slice the grape tomatoes in half, place on a parchment-lined cookie sheet, lightly drizzle with balsamic vinegar, and top with minced garlic and a pinch of sea salt. Bake in the oven for about 40 minutes. The tomatoes should be soft and shriveled but not completely dried. These can be done 1 day ahead and stored in the fridge.

3 Slice the halloumi about ¼-inch thick, then cut each slice in half. Place the flour in a bowl, add the halloumi, and toss to coat evenly with the flour. Tip into a fine sieve and shake to remove any excess flour. Heat the grapeseed oil in a nonstick pan set on medium heat. Fry the pieces of halloumi on both sides until golden brown, about 3 to 5 minutes total.

4 While the cheese is frying, cut the buns in half and slather the bottom halves (don't be cheap) with both the onion jam and mayo. Top with the warm halloumi, a few tomato halves, some lettuce leaves, and the top halves of the buns. To serve, pierce a cornichon with a fancy skewer and skewer through each slider. Repeat with remaining sliders.

NOTE

Halloumi cheese originated in Cyprus, but is commonly served throughout the Middle East. It can be made from sheep's milk, goat's milk, or a mixture. Miraculously, this cheese can be fried or grilled without melting and losing its shape.

Pesto Caprese Cups

In order for a cocktail party to be a roaring success, you must include vegetarian options. Don't even consider the crudité platter with dip—we have far more creativity than that! The cuteness factor in this starter comes from the pearl bocconcini balls, which you can find at Italian delis. Any leftovers can be tossed into your dinner salad later in the week.

---

1 Preheat your oven to 350°F.

2 Cut the crusts from the bread. Using a rolling pin, roll the bread as thin as possible. Using your cookie cutter, cut circles out of the bread. Brush both sides of the circles lightly with olive oil and press into the mini muffin pan, ensuring you press into all sides of the cavities so the bread cups bake open. Bake for 8 to 10 minutes or until golden brown. Remove and set aside to cool. The bread cups can be prepared 2 days ahead of time and stored in an airtight container.

3 Cut the tomatoes into quarters and set aside. Pinch all the small baby leaves from the bunch of basil and set aside. Reserve the rest of the bunch for another use (such as the Pesto recipe on page 170).

4 To serve, spoon 1 to 2 teaspoons of pesto into each baked bread cup. Using the back of a tiny sugar spoon, spread the pesto up the sides of each cup. Set the tomato quarters on their tips to fill the cup, making sure you mix up the colors. Add five or six of the pearl bocconcini to each cup, then decorate with the basil leaves and a scattering of the toasted pine nuts. Finish with a sprinkle of fleur de sel and a grind of fresh pepper.

NOTE
There are many sizes of bocconcini (mozzarella balls), the pearls being the smallest, about the size of a small pea.
If you can't find these, cut up what you can find into small pea-sized portions.

INGREDIENTS
8 slices white bread
Extra virgin olive oil, for brushing
1 cup yellow grape tomatoes
1 cup red grape tomatoes
1 bunch fresh basil leaves
1 cup Pesto (page 170; or use store-bought)
1 cup pearl bocconcini (see note)
½ cup toasted pine nuts (see page 166)
Fleur de sel and freshly ground pepper

SPECIAL EQUIPMENT
24-cup mini muffin pan
Round cookie cutter, ¼-inch larger in diameter than top of muffin cavity

MAKES 24 CAPRESE CUPS

Mini Tomato Tartes Tatin

Tatin does not always have to be sweet. I have taken this upside-down dessert, shrunk it into a mini tarte, and transformed sweet to savory. Baked upside down, the balsamic glaze bathes the tomatoes in a glorious oozing sweetness while the crust crisps into a flaky puff for the base. This is beyond culinary magic.

---

1 Preheat your oven to 400°F.

2 Sprinkle some flour on a clean work surface. Roll the pastry out until about ¼ inch thick. Sprinkle all over with ½ cup of the cheese and all of the smoked paprika. Fold the dough in half to cover the cheese and paprika. Roll the entire piece of pastry to about ¾ inch thick. Using your cookie cutter, cut out 24 circles.

3 Put ½ tablespoon of balsamic glaze into each muffin cavity. Place a grape tomato half on top of the glaze, cut side down. Top with a few strips of the sun-dried tomatoes, a pinch of the fresh thyme leaves, and a generous teaspoon of Parmesan cheese, and finish with a good grind of pepper.

4 Place a puff pastry circle into each cavity and bake in the oven for 10 to 12 minutes, or until golden brown. Remove from the oven and let rest for 5 minutes before carefully removing and inverting the tartes onto a serving plate.

5 Serve hot or at room temperature.

INGREDIENTS

Unbleached all-purpose flour, for rolling the pastry

1 package (½ lb) frozen all-butter puff pastry, thawed

1¼ cups freshly grated Parmesan cheese

1 Tbsp sweet or hot smoked Spanish paprika (see page 5)

¾ cup Balsamic Glaze (page 168; or use store-bought)

12 sun-dried tomato halves, julienned

12 grape tomatoes, halved

¼ cup fresh thyme leaves

Freshly ground pepper

SPECIAL EQUIPMENT

24-cup mini muffin pan

Round fluted cookie cutter, ½-inch larger in diameter than top of muffin cavity

MAKES 24 TARTES

Prosciutto Cups with Cheese Bread Stuffing

INGREDIENTS

12 slices Italian prosciutto, cut into quarters

⅓ cup coffee cream (18%)

1 large free-range egg

1 large shallot, finely minced

1 large clove garlic, minced

1 Tbsp fresh thyme leaves

1 tsp chili paste (see page 4)

2 cups finely cubed day-old bread (I like to use an Italian cheese loaf; see note)

1 cup pitted, chopped kalamata olives

½ cup pine nuts

½ cup grated Emmentaler cheese

½ cup cubed Italian Gorgonzola cheese

⅓ cup dried cranberries

⅓ cup finely chopped fresh parsley

SPECIAL EQUIPMENT

24-cup mini muffin pan

MAKES 24 PROSCIUTTO CUPS

This tasty little cup of Mediterranean flavors will steal the party from most pastry-based appetizers. The prosciutto base filled with an amazing combination of savory, salty, and sweet will make your taste buds give in for just one more.

---

1 Preheat your oven to 400°F.

2 Line each muffin cavity with two pieces of the prosciutto. Using your fingers, push the prosciutto against the pan so it adheres. Set aside.

3 In a large bowl, whisk the cream and egg together, then add the shallot, garlic, thyme, and chili paste and whisk well to combine. Stir in the bread cubes, olives, pine nuts, both cheeses, cranberries, and parsley. Mix well.

4 Spoon the mixture into the prosciutto-lined muffin cups and bake in the oven for 15 minutes, or until golden brown. The prosciutto will be nice and crisp, while the filling oozes with cheese and flavor. Serve hot or at room temperature.

NOTE

When cutting the bread cubes, make sure you cut them small enough to fit the cups.

Hot Cheese Soufflés

The mere mention of soufflé frightens even the most seasoned of home cooks. In all honesty, if you can beat egg whites, you can make soufflé. That sounds rather silly, but it is the truth. However, the simple overbeating of egg whites will be the death and deflation of your creation. The whites need to be soft and pillowy. A simple base folded into the soft whites, met with a hot oven, produces your personal culinary elation. That is what a soufflé does for your cooking psyche.

INGREDIENTS

3 Tbsp unsalted butter

3 Tbsp unbleached all-purpose flour

1 Tbsp Dijon mustard

Pinch of sweet smoked Spanish paprika (see page 5)

1 cup whole milk (2% works too)

4 large free-range eggs, separated

½ cup grated Gruyère cheese

¼ cup freshly grated Parmesan cheese

½ tsp ground five-pepper blend (see note)

3 free-range egg whites

¼ tsp cream of tartar

1 Preheat your oven to 375°F.

2 For the base, in a heavy-bottomed pot over medium heat, melt the butter, then stir in the flour and let it cook for about 2 minutes to remove its raw taste; continue to stir as it cooks. Add the mustard and paprika, then slowly whisk in the milk until the base is smooth and creamy. Add the four egg yolks one at a time, whisking well after each addition. Stir in the cheeses along with the pepper blend. This base can be made several hours ahead up to this point and set aside in the pot.

Let cool, cover the mixture with a piece of plastic wrap pressed directly on the surface to prevent a skin from forming, and place in the fridge.

3 About half an hour before serving time, place all seven egg whites in the bowl of a stand mixer fitted with a whisk attachment, or use a handheld electric mixer in a large bowl. Slowly beat the whites for 1 minute, sprinkle in the cream of tartar, and continue whisking until the whites are soft and peaks form when the whisk attachment is lifted, about 5 to 7 minutes. Take care not to overbeat.

4 Scoop about 1 cup of the beaten whites and gently fold into the reserved base to lighten it. Then gently fold in the remaining whites, again taking care not to overfold. Distribute the soufflé batter evenly among the six ramekins.

5 Bake for 15 to 20 minutes, or until the soufflés have risen over the tops of their dishes. Do not be tempted to open the oven; this is a sure deflator.

6 When the soufflés are done, remove from the oven and serve immediately.

SPECIAL EQUIPMENT
Six 6 oz ramekins

MAKES 6 SOUFFLÉS

NOTES

This is a perfect starter to any sit-down dinner when you want to show off a tiny bit (or maybe a big bit). Just do it!

Five-pepper blend is composed of four different peppercorns—white, green, black, and pink—and the fifth component is actually allspice, used to give an almost aromatic finish to the pepper mix. If you do not have it, it is okay to use black pepper instead.

Mini Tomato Soups with Crispy Parmesan Tuiles

INGREDIENTS

2 Tbsp extra virgin olive oil

2 Tbsp unsalted butter

1 small yellow onion, diced
  (about 1 heaping cup)

½ cup peeled and diced
  sweet potato

1 large clove garlic, minced

1 can (28 oz) San Marzano
  tomatoes

2 cups chicken stock

2 sprigs fresh thyme

Sea salt and freshly ground
  pepper

12 large fresh basil leaves,
  cut into chiffonade (see
  note)

Parmesan Tuiles (page 167)

**MAKES TWELVE 4 OZ
SERVINGS**

This soup looks so inviting when presented as a small appetizer portion, and it is a perfect starter for a sit-down dinner. I sometimes serve it in little enamel mugs, as pictured, but I also love to pick from the mismatched collection of assorted bone china teacups I inherited from my mom. Either way, the cute factor impresses everyone. As with any soup, this tastes great (if not better) the next day.

---

1 Place the oil and butter in a stainless-steel pot over high heat. Add the onion, sweet potato, and garlic. Stir to combine, then cover. Turn the heat to medium and let the mixture sweat until the onion and sweet potato are soft, but not brown, about 12 to 15 minutes. Stir in the tomatoes (with their juices), chicken stock, and thyme, and let the soup simmer, covered, for 20 minutes.

2 Remove the thyme sprigs and, using a blender or food processor, purée the soup in batches, making sure no lumps remain. Return the puréed soup to the pot, and season with the sea salt and pepper to taste. Ladle into small cups, sprinkle each with a few shreds of the basil chiffonade, and crown with a Parmesan tuile.

NOTES

Chiffonade is a term used for finely cut or shredded leafy herbs such as basil, mint, or sage. To achieve a chiffonade, flatten each leaf and stack on top of each other, then tightly roll the stack and finely slice. This will produce a lovely stack of shredded herbs.

This would also be fun to serve in shooter glasses for a cocktail party. This recipe makes enough for twenty-four 2 oz shooter portions. If topping with Parmesan Tuiles, make them half the size as suggested in the recipe on page 167 to make 24 tuiles.

Clockwise from top: Quinoa Tabbouleh (page 81); Purple Peruvian Potato Salad (page 80); Quinoa Salad with Roasted Veg and Hazelnut Dressing (page 76)

Salads

To cook is to be creative. It's all about tasting, experimenting and adding a personal touch here and there. Salads are a great place to do just that, especially now that they have moved far beyond the boring, basic side salad that was our loyal standby for years. With salads you can be truly spontaneous, and throw together the ingredients you have on hand without stressing too much about getting things exactly right.

For the salad recipes in these pages, I've focused on flavor and texture combinations, and bringing creative passion into their preparation. Using fresh, exciting, and even exotic ingredients will take your salads to new heights, and transform your entire meal. I want you to experience the pride of grilling a humble cob of corn, shearing the kernels, and then combining them with black beans, diced avocado, spices, and fresh herbs to create a simple yet colorful dish of delish. I want your salads to be the cheerleaders for every main you present. I want your buffet spread and summer barbecue salads to light up your table with excitement. Presentation is paramount, as we always eat with our eyes first.

Salads are generally the easiest dishes to execute when entertaining, as so much can be prepared ahead of time. The dressings in these recipes can be made in advance and will keep refrigerated for up to 5 days, depending on the ingredients. This chapter is full of delicious ideas and unique presentations that await your execution. Get ready for your guests to applaud your new repertoire . . . and eat happily ever after!

Warm Maple Bacon Spinach Salad

INGREDIENTS

6 thin slices bacon, diced,
    drippings reserved
1 package (5.29 oz) fresh
    shimeji mushrooms, root
    ends trimmed (see note)
Fleur de sel and freshly
    ground pepper
6 heaping cups fresh
    spinach leaves, stems
    removed
½ cup crumbled goat
    cheese (garnish)

DRESSING

3 Tbsp reserved bacon
    drippings
½ large shallot, finely minced
    (about 2 heaping Tbsp)
1 Tbsp aged sherry vinegar
2 tsp Dijon mustard
⅓ cup extra virgin olive oil
1 Tbsp pure Canadian maple
    syrup

SERVES 4 TO 6

Back in the 1980s, warm spinach salad was *the* go-to dish. Since then, I have eaten a multitude of spinach salads embellished with fatty bits of bacon and other assorted toppings—all rather unmemorable. The secret to getting it right lies in ensuring that the spinach leaves are not stone cold, but at room temperature, so that when you pour the warm dressing over top, it creates the perfect balance. This salad is a good summer barbecue companion, as spinach holds up much longer than other salad greens.

———

1 In a medium pan over medium heat, fry the bacon until all the pieces are crisp and browned—no fatty bits, please. Remove the bacon from the pan and transfer to a plate lined with paper towel to absorb any excess fat. Set aside.

2 Measure out 3 tablespoons of the bacon drippings and discard the rest. To make the dressing, place the drippings back in the same pan and add the shallot. Turn the heat to low and let the shallot infuse into the bacon fat until soft, about 5 minutes. Turn off the heat and whisk in the sherry vinegar and mustard. Once the dressing is cool, add the olive oil and maple syrup. The dressing can be prepared up to this point 1 day ahead.

3 When you are ready to serve, heat the dressing on low and add the mushrooms, warming through until the mushrooms are soft. Season with fleur de sel and fresh pepper to taste.

4 Place the spinach leaves in a bowl. Pour the warm dressing over top and toss to coat all the leaves. Transfer the salad to your serving plate (see note). Sprinkle the reserved bacon bits over top, then the crumbled goat cheese, and serve immediately.

NOTES

Shimeji mushrooms hail from Japan and grow, cluster-like, in hot houses. Most good grocers stock them in both white and brown. If these are unavailable, you can use small button mushrooms instead.

Choose a long, rather than round, plate when plating. I like that this allows the beautiful colors and garnish to shine, rather than burying them in a bowl.

Shaved Garden Slaw

This is my version of a summer slaw, screaming with flavor and multiple textures, but with no purple cabbage or pedestrian carrots. It goes perfectly with ribs of any kind, as the tartness of the salad offsets the richness of the ribs. Crunch on!

INGREDIENTS

1 medium head Italian radicchio, cored and shredded

1 small head napa cabbage, finely shredded

1 large fresh fennel bulb, cored and finely shaved

1 bunch kale, stems and ribs removed, finely shredded

1 package (4 oz) snow peas, strings removed and sliced on the diagonal

½ bunch fresh cilantro, leaves only

1 cup toasted pumpkin seeds (see page 166)

1 cup dried cranberries

DRESSING

½ cup mayonnaise (I like Hellmann's)

⅓ cup sour cream

¼ cup plain yogurt (I like Liberté)

2 cloves garlic, minced

1 medium shallot, finely minced

3 Tbsp mango vinegar (see note)

2 Tbsp Dijon mustard

1 Tbsp chili paste (see page 4)

Sea salt and freshly ground pepper

SERVES 6 TO 8

1 Whisk all the dressing ingredients together in a bowl. Taste for seasoning, and adjust to suit your preference. Let the dressing sit for about an hour to allow the flavors to develop.

2 Toss all the vegetables together, including the cilantro leaves. Pour the dressing over top and mix to combine. Do not overdress.

3 To serve, transfer the slaw to your serving bowl and top with the pumpkin seeds and cranberries.

NOTE

If mango vinegar is not available, you can use white balsamic instead (see page 4).

Grilled Corn, Black Bean, and Avocado Salad

This colorful salad is perfect for a simple buffet, and leftovers make a wonderful lunch the next day.

———————

1 Peel the corn cobs and grill them on the barbecue or in a grill pan over medium-low heat, about 15 to 20 minutes. Turn the cobs every few minutes; you want them evenly browned on all sides. Remove and cool.

2 Strip the kernels from the cobs: stand each one on a plate or shallow pan, hold the tip firmly and cut the kernels from top to bottom. Place the kernels in a bowl, and add the beans and cilantro.

3 To make the dressing, place the shallot, garlic, chili paste, rice vinegar, soy sauce, sesame oil, mustard powder, lime zest and juice, and pinch of sugar in a bowl. Whisk all the ingredients together; then, in a slow, steady stream, drizzle in the oil, whisking the entire time. The dressing will come together in a smooth, creamy consistency. Season with sea salt and fresh pepper to suit your taste.

4 Pour the dressing over the corn, beans, and cilantro and toss to coat well. Adjust the seasoning with fleur de sel and ground pepper to taste.

5 Transfer to a serving platter lined with lettuce leaves, if using. Just before serving, sprinkle the avocado cubes and goat cheese over top. Do not toss or the avocado will become mushy.

NOTE

If fresh corn is not available, substitute with two 14-ounce cans of corn kernels, drained and rinsed. Drain well, place the corn in a cast iron or fry pan, along with 1 tablespoon of roasted grapeseed oil, and cook it over medium-high heat until browned, about 10 minutes. Periodically shake the pan to encourage even browning. Cool and add to the salad.

INGREDIENTS

5 fresh corn cobs (see note)
2 cups cooked or canned black beans, drained and rinsed
½ bunch fresh cilantro, coarsely chopped
Fleur de sel and freshly ground pepper
Butter lettuce leaves (optional)
2 avocados, diced (garnish)
1 cup crumbled goat cheese or feta cheese (garnish)

DRESSING

1 large shallot, finely minced
2 small cloves garlic, minced
1 Tbsp chili paste (see page 4)
1 Tbsp rice vinegar
1 Tbsp soy sauce
1 Tbsp toasted sesame oil (see page 5)
1 Tbsp dry mustard powder
Zest of 1 small lime
1 tsp fresh lime juice
Pinch of sugar
⅔ cup roasted grapeseed oil
Sea salt and freshly ground pepper

SERVES 6 TO 8

Quinoa Salad with Roasted Veg and Hazelnut Dressing

INGREDIENTS

1 cup black quinoa (see note, page 81)

Pinch of sea salt

1 medium yellow pepper (or buy roasted peppers in a jar and skip the roasting step)

12 spears asparagus

Extra virgin olive oil, for roasting and frying

1 medium sweet onion, diced

Kosher salt

1 cup frozen shelled edamame beans

1 avocado, diced into ½-inch chunks

Super grain, super food, and super protein that tastes super good! Roasted vegetables bring color and vibrancy to the quinoa. Poached or grilled salmon is a perfect main to pair with this salad. Any leftovers are perfect for lunch.

1 Preheat your oven to 400°F.

2 Whisk together all the dressing ingredients except for the oils and the salt and pepper. Slowly drizzle in the oils and whisk until the dressing is thick and smooth. Season with salt and pepper to taste. Set aside.

3 Bring 2 cups of water to a boil, then add the quinoa and a pinch of salt. Turn the heat down and simmer, covered, for about 12 minutes or until all the liquid is absorbed. Fluff with a fork and set aside to cool.

4 Meanwhile, prepare the vegetables. Halve, seed, and slice the pepper and snap the tough ends off the asparagus. Place the slices and spears on a cookie sheet along with a light drizzle of olive oil just to coat. Roast for 10 minutes, or until browned, then remove from the oven, cool, and cut into pieces.

5 While the vegetables are roasting, heat olive oil over medium heat in a fry pan and cook the onion until soft. Set aside. Blanch the edamame in boiling water seasoned with kosher salt until cooked, about 3 to 4 minutes, then drain and refresh in ice water to preserve the color. Once cooled, drain well.

6 In a large bowl, mix together the yellow pepper, asparagus, onion, edamame, avocado, grape tomatoes, and herbs. Add the cooked quinoa, then pour the dressing over top. Toss to mix, ensuring the dressing coats all the grains.

7 Transfer to a serving platter and garnish with the toasted hazelnuts.

1 cup grape tomatoes, halved
1 cup fresh Italian parsley leaves
1 cup fresh basil chiffonade (see note, page 66)
3 Tbsp snipped fresh chives
1 cup chopped toasted hazelnuts (garnish; see page 166)

DRESSING
1 large clove garlic, minced
2 Tbsp champagne vinegar
1 Tbsp Dijon mustard
½ cup hazelnut oil (see page 5)
¼ cup extra virgin olive oil
Sea salt and freshly ground pepper

SERVES 6 TO 8

Greek Salad Skewers

Everyone loves Greek salad, so here is a skewered form of the traditional classic! It's perfect for buffets or plated for individual servings. Big made small.

_____

INGREDIENTS

Twenty-four 6-inch fancy skewers
24 grape tomatoes
4 Lebanese cucumbers, cut into twenty-four ½-inch pieces (see note, page 107)
1 large white sweet onion, cut into twenty-four ½-inch squares
2 large red peppers, cut into twenty-four ½-inch squares
24 pitted kalamata olives
1 tub (1 lb) feta cheese, drained and cut into twenty-four ½-inch cubes
1 head butter lettuce

DRESSING

½ cup extra virgin olive oil
3 Tbsp fresh lemon juice
2 tsp dried oregano
Fleur de sel and freshly ground pepper

MAKES 24 SKEWERS

1 Skewer the veggies, olives, and feta, using one piece of each per skewer. Lay the completed skewers on a shallow tray.

2 Mix all dressing ingredients together and pour the dressing over the skewers. Let them marinate at room temperature for about 20 minutes. You can also prepare them a few hours before serving and let them marinate in the refrigerator.

3 Just before serving, cut the root end off the head of lettuce. Gently peel off the leaves one by one to form lettuce cups, being careful not to tear them. Wash and blot dry in a clean kitchen towel. To serve, lay the lettuce cups on a serving plate, trimming the leaves so they are all the same size. Lay the colorful skewers on the leaves. If you are doing individual plating, use one lettuce leaf per serving and four skewers per person.

Purple Peruvian Potato Salad

INGREDIENTS

Kosher salt

2 cups fresh sweet baby
    peas (see note)

3 lb purple Peruvian
    potatoes (see note)

DRESSING

2 Tbsp Dijon mustard

2 Tbsp tarragon or white
    balsamic vinegar (see
    page 4)

⅓ cup roasted grapeseed oil

⅓ cup extra virgin olive oil

2 Tbsp chopped fresh
    tarragon

2 Tbsp snipped fresh chives

1 Tbsp chopped fresh mint

Fleur de sel and freshly
    ground pepper

SERVES 6

Photo on page 68

So many types of potatoes and so little time to eat them all! Begin with this intensely colored purple Peruvian variety. The texture is smooth, not grainy, and consequently makes for a luscious and vibrant potato salad like no other. Not to worry, though, if purple isn't your color or you can't find them. Any baby potato or fingerling will do.

---

1 Blanch the peas in boiling salted water for 1 to 2 minutes, then refresh in an ice bath, drain, and set aside.

2 Make the dressing by placing the mustard in a bowl. Add the vinegar and slowly whisk in the oils, then add the tarragon, chives, mint, and finally the fleur de sel and pepper to suit your taste. Set aside.

3 Peel and quarter the potatoes. Place them in a pot, fill with water to barely cover, add some kosher salt, and bring to a boil. Cook the potatoes until soft but not mushy, about 15 to 20 minutes; al dente does not work with potatoes. Drain and place the potatoes in your serving bowl, then pour the dressing over top while the potatoes are hot; this allows the dressing to be absorbed. Wait until the salad is completely cool before adjusting the seasoning.

4 When the salad is ready to serve, sprinkle in the peas and toss lightly to combine.

NOTES

If fresh peas are not available, sub in the frozen "sweetlets," the tiny peas in the freezer section.

Purple Peruvians can be sourced at good produce stores. They also come in small nugget size; choose these if they're available, but don't bother peeling them.

Quinoa Tabbouleh

I have taken the refreshing Lebanese flavors of the classic tabbouleh salad and replaced the traditionally used bulgur wheat with the hugely popular quinoa. This salad is protein-rich and very colorful.

---

1 Wash and drain the quinoa, then place it in a pot with 2 cups of water. Bring to a boil and cook, covered, for 15 minutes, or until all the water is absorbed. Remove from heat, fluff with a fork, and let cool.

2 While the quinoa is cooling, place the cucumbers, tomatoes, parsley, cilantro, mint, and green onions in a bowl. Set aside.

3 Prepare the dressing by whisking together the olive oil, lemon juice, garlic, and preserved lemon rind, then season to taste with the kosher salt and pepper. Pour the dressing over the cooled quinoa, add the prepared vegetables and herbs, and stir to combine. Transfer to a serving dish.

NOTES

Quinoa can be purchased white, black, or red. The cooking time is the same, so you can mix the colors together. Quinoa hails from Peru, Bolivia, Ecuador, and Chile. One of the oldest grains in history, it was first domesticated for human consumption over 3,000 years ago.

It is important to finely mince the herbs, since they need to blend into the grains and not be coarse.

INGREDIENTS

1 cup quinoa (see note)

3 Lebanese cucumbers, diced (see note, page 107)

2 cups grape tomatoes, halved

1 bunch fresh Italian parsley, finely minced (see note)

1 cup finely minced fresh cilantro

½ cup finely minced fresh mint

4 green onions, thinly sliced

DRESSING

⅔ cup extra virgin olive oil

Juice of ½ lemon

1 clove garlic, minced

1 Tbsp finely chopped preserved lemon rind (see page 4)

Kosher salt and freshly ground pepper

SERVES 8

Photo on page 68

Clara's Pickled Vegetable Salad

INGREDIENTS

5 cups trimmed cauliflower, broken into tiny florets

5 cups trimmed broccoli, broken into tiny florets

4 stalks celery, trimmed and diced into ¼-inch pieces

2 medium red peppers, cored and diced into ¼-inch pieces

2 medium carrots, peeled and diced into ¼-inch pieces

1 large sweet onion, diced into ¼-inch pieces

MARINADE

1 cup plain white vinegar

1 cup berry sugar (see note)

¾ cup roasted grapeseed oil

½ cup white balsamic vinegar (see page 4)

1 ½ Tbsp kosher salt

Freshly ground pepper

SERVES 8 TO 10

My mom, Clara, was famous for her Elvis impersonations, naughty Christmas Poem, and summer patio parties. This salad was a classic she served all summer long. No one ever made it but her, not because of difficulty, but simply because of the time she took to make sure every little floret was even and perfect. You can get the same pleasure from this salad without taking too much time to perfect and minimize the tiny florets as Clara did. This one is for you, Mom!

1 For the marinade, warm half of the white vinegar in a saucepan over medium-low heat, add the sugar, and turn off the heat. The purpose is to simply dissolve the sugar. Once the sugar is dissolved, remove from the stove and cool. As soon as it cools, add the remaining white vinegar, grapeseed oil, balsamic, salt, and pepper to taste. Stir to combine, then set aside while you prepare the vegetables.

2 Place the cauliflower and the broccoli in a large bowl. Toss in the celery, peppers, carrots, and sweet onion.

3 Pour the cooled marinade over the vegetables, cover the bowl with plastic wrap, and refrigerate for at least 12 hours, or overnight.

4 To serve, drain off and discard the marinade and place the vegetables in a clear glass bowl to show off their color (or see note). The salad will keep well in the refrigerator for 3 to 4 days.

NOTES

Berry sugar is a superfine form of granulated sugar, easily purchased at grocery stores everywhere. If you cannot source it, substitute with regular granulated sugar.

For a fancier presentation, use whole cabbage leaves to line a serving dish and spoon the salad into the leaves.

Haricot Vert and Pea Salad

INGREDIENTS

Kosher salt

1 package (about 14 oz)
  skinny green beans
  (haricots verts), washed
  and trimmed

1 package (9 oz) frozen
  shelled edamame beans

1 package (8 oz) snap peas,
  strings removed

2 cups arugula, spinach, or
  watercress leaves

½ cup fresh mint chiffonade
  (garnish; see note, page 66)

DRESSING

1 large shallot, finely minced

2 cloves garlic, minced

1 Tbsp grated ginger (see
  note, page 94)

1 Tbsp fresh lime zest

3 Tbsp fresh lime juice

1 Tbsp chili paste (see page 4)

2 tsp Dijon mustard

1 tsp liquid honey (see note,
  page 109)

½ cup roasted grapeseed oil

Sea salt and freshly ground
  pepper

SERVES 6 TO 8

This vibrant green salad is a welcome change from lettuce. It can be prepped a day in advance and assembled just before serving. Haricot verts are the skinny French version of green beans. Try to find them; they are worth the search. The vibrant green-on-green color of this salad is a perfect addition to any summer barbecue.

1 Fill a large pot with water and bring to a boil. Once boiling, add some kosher salt and blanch the green beans for about 3 minutes, or until al dente. Immediately transfer the beans to a large bowl of ice water to stop the cooking process and to preserve their color. Do the same with the edamame beans and again with the snap peas. Do not cook them all together, as their cooking times and sizes vary. The edamame will take about 3 to 4 minutes, and the snap peas about 2 minutes, depending on how cooked you like your vegetables.

2 Drain the vegetables from their ice baths and transfer to a clean kitchen towel (not paper towel). Slice the snap peas on the diagonal. Wrap the vegetables up in the kitchen towel and chill in the towel until ready to serve.

3 For the dressing, combine the shallot, garlic, ginger, lime zest and juice, chili paste, mustard, and honey in a small bowl. Slowly pour in the oil while whisking, then season to taste with salt and pepper. Set aside until serving time. This can be made up to 2 days in advance and refrigerated.

4 To serve, line a platter with arugula, spinach, or watercress leaves. Place the green beans, edamame beans, and snap peas in a bowl, pour the dressing over, and toss well to coat everything evenly. Transfer to the prepared platter and sprinkle the mint chiffonade over top.

Fruited Couscous Salad

Couscous is one of the easiest things to make, but it is the addition of interesting flavor combinations that elevates this dish to the next level. This works well with any lamb or chicken dish.

---

1 Place the stock in a pot, bring to a boil, add the couscous, and remove from heat. Let sit with the lid on for 10 minutes.

2 Meanwhile, place the cranberries, currants, and apricots in a medium bowl and pour in 2 cups of hot water to cover the fruit. Let the fruit sit in the hot water for about 5 minutes. This plumps the fruit and rids it of any surplus sugar crystals that tend to cling to dried fruit. Drain well.

3 Mix the lemon oil, lemon juice, and turmeric together, and add fleur de sel to taste. Pour over the couscous and fluff with a large fork. Add the drained fruit, mint, cilantro, and pumpkin seeds. Fluff again with the fork to keep the couscous nice and light. Transfer to a colorful tagine or dish and serve warm or at room temperature.

NOTE
If you do not have lemon-infused olive oil, simply add 1 teaspoon of fresh lemon zest per ¼ cup of olive oil to give you that subtle lemon essence.

INGREDIENTS

2 cups chicken or vegetable stock

1 ¾ cups couscous

⅓ cup chopped dried cranberries

⅓ cup dried currants

⅓ cup chopped dried apricots

½ cup lemon-infused extra virgin olive oil (see note)

Juice of ½ lemon

1 tsp ground turmeric

Fleur de sel

⅓ cup julienned fresh mint

⅓ cup torn fresh cilantro leaves

¼ cup toasted pumpkin seeds (see page 166)

SERVES 6

Southwest Salad Baskets

These individual salad baskets are a cute alternative to a bowl. This is a perfect salad for lunch or featured on a buffet.

INGREDIENTS

3 Tbsp roasted grapeseed oil

1 tsp ground cumin

1 tsp kosher salt

Twelve 6-inch flour tortillas

1 small head iceberg lettuce

1 cup cooked or canned black beans, drained and rinsed

¾ cup pitted, sliced kalamata olives

10 grape tomatoes, quartered

1 medium jicama, peeled and diced into ¼-inch pieces (optional; see note)

½ small sweet onion, thinly sliced

½ cup grated Monterey Jack cheese

½ cup grated aged cheddar cheese

10 pickled jalapeño pepper slices, chopped (optional)

1 avocado, diced into ¼-inch pieces

1 cup coarsely chopped fresh cilantro leaves

1 cup your favorite salsa

½ cup sour cream (garnish)

Cilantro leaves (garnish)

SPECIAL EQUIPMENT

12-cup muffin pan

Round cookie cutter, ½-inch larger in diameter than top of muffin cavity

MAKES 12 SALAD BASKETS

1 Preheat your oven to 350°F.

2 Mix the oil, cumin, and salt together in a small bowl and set aside. Lay the tortillas on your work surface. Using your cookie cutter, cut out 12 circles. Lightly brush both sides of each circle with the oil mixture.

3 Press the circles into the muffin cavities, pressing on all sides so they stick and form a cup. This step is important because you want the cavities to remain open and not cave in during the baking process.

4 Bake for about 8 minutes, or until crisp and golden brown. Remove and cool. The tortilla baskets can be made up to 2 days ahead and stored in an airtight container.

5 For the salad filling, finely shred the lettuce and transfer to a large bowl. Add the beans, olives, tomatoes, jicama (if using), onion, both types of cheese, and jalapeños, if using. Toss to combine.

6 When you are ready to serve, set the baskets on your serving tray. Place the diced avocado in the bowl with the veggies, then add the cilantro, pour the salsa over, and toss to mix. Mix lightly to avoid smashing the avocado. Carefully spoon into the prepared baskets and garnish each with a dollop of sour cream and a cilantro leaf.

NOTE

Jicama originates in Mexico, and can be found in Latin
or Asian markets. It has a brown skin, and a juicy, moist
crunch almost like a savory apple (though unlike an apple,
it does not brown once peeled and cut). It can be eaten as a
snack, used in salsas, or, as in this case, added as a unique
ingredient to salad.

Sweet Pea, Edamame, and Burrata Salad

INGREDIENTS

Kosher salt

3 cups frozen shelled
    edamame beans

1 package (1 lb) frozen peas
    (the small "sweetlet"
    variety)

Fleur de sel and freshly
    ground pepper

1 cup fresh pea shoots

1 ball (8 oz) burrata cheese,
    left whole or cut into
    walnut-sized bites (see
    recipe introduction,
    page 97)

DRESSING

2 Tbsp tarragon or white
    balsamic vinegar (see
    page 4)

1 Tbsp finely chopped
    preserved lemon rind
    (see page 4)

1 Tbsp Dijon mustard

½ cup extra virgin olive oil

½ cup finely chopped fresh
    Italian parsley

Pinch of sugar

Sea salt and freshly ground
    pepper

SERVES 6

The combination of sweet peas, firm edamame, and creamy burrata ranks this salad at the top of my list. When it comes to cheese, everyone knows cheddar, mozza, and jack, but burrata is the new cheese kid on the block. Look for it in good delis and gourmet stores.

---

1 Blanch the edamame in boiling water seasoned with kosher salt for 3 to 4 minutes, then drain and refresh in an ice bath. Once cooled, drain well, and set aside.

2 Blanch the frozen peas in boiling salted water for 2 minutes, then refresh in an ice bath, drain, and set aside.

3 To make the dressing, in a small bowl, whisk together the vinegar, preserved lemon rind, and mustard. Slowly whisk in the olive oil until the dressing is thick and smooth. Add the parsley, pinch of sugar, and salt and pepper to taste.

4 Combine the peas and edamame beans, pour the dressing over top, and toss to coat. Adjust seasoning with fleur de sel and pepper to taste.

5 Transfer the mixture to a serving platter. Line the edge of the platter with the pea shoots, and garnish with the burrata.

NOTE
Nothing really compares to the delicious decadence of burrata, but you can substitute fresh buffalo mozzarella or goat cheese in a pinch.

White Salad

Perhaps this isn't the best-sounding name, but this white salad looks and tastes amazing. When a small dinner starter salad is needed, this will impress your guests with elegance and superb taste.

---

1 Cut the hearts of palm lengthwise into eighths, transfer to a paper-towel-lined plate, and chill until ready to serve. This step can be done the night before, if desired.

2 Cut the fennel in half, remove the woody core, and slice thinly with a sharp knife or a mandoline. Set aside and chill. This can be done in advance if desired, but if preparing several hours before, submerge the fennel in a bowl of cold water to prevent browning.

3 Cut the endives in half, remove the cores, and thinly julienne. Set aside and chill.

4 For the dressing, place the mustard in a small bowl, whisk in the white balsamic vinegar, then drizzle in the olive oil in a slow, steady stream, whisking the entire time. The dressing will come together in a beautiful, smooth, creamy mass. Set aside until ready to serve. It may separate while sitting, so give it a quick whisk before serving.

5 To serve, toss all of the chilled vegetables together in a large bowl, slowly drizzle the prepared dressing over top, and toss very gently to coat. Do not be aggressive or overdress, as the ingredients are delicate. Portion on chilled white plates, sprinkle with pinches of fleur de sel and white pepper to taste, and garnish with the blue cheese and toasted pine nuts.

INGREDIENTS

1 can (14 oz) hearts of palm, drained and rinsed (see note)

1 small bulb fresh fennel

2 heads Belgian endive

Fleur de sel and freshly ground white pepper

1 cup crumbled blue cheese, such as Stilton or Roquefort (garnish)

½ cup toasted pine nuts (garnish; see page 166)

DRESSING

2 tsp Dijon mustard

¼ cup white balsamic vinegar (see page 4)

⅔ cup extra virgin olive oil

SERVES 6

NOTE

Hearts of palm are the early shoots of the palm tree that emerge every spring. They are purchased canned. They have a delicate flavor and a soft, not crunchy, texture.

Soba Sesame Salad

INGREDIENTS

Kosher salt

1 package (8 oz) soba
    noodles

1 lb asparagus (thin spears
    work best here)

1 cup julienned carrots

1 cup julienned sweet onion

1 medium red pepper,
    julienned

1 cup toasted sesame seeds

1 cup fresh cilantro leaves
    (garnish)

DRESSING

1 large shallot, finely minced

4 Tbsp soy sauce

3 Tbsp toasted sesame oil
    (see page 5)

2 Tbsp rice vinegar

1 Tbsp grated ginger (see
    note)

1 Tbsp liquid honey (see
    note, page 109)

½ cup roasted grapeseed oil

Sea salt and freshly ground
    pepper

SERVES 6

I love a good pasta salad that includes lots of veggies along with the noodles. The nutty flavor of soba provides a departure from regular pasta, and the Asian-inspired dressing marries well with grilled meats for a main meal.

---

1 Cook the soba noodles according to package instructions in a large pot of boiling salted water. Drain well and rinse immediately in cold water to prevent sticking. Set aside to continue draining.

2 Snap the tough ends off the asparagus. In a pot fitted with a steamer, steam the asparagus until al dente, about 5 to 7 minutes, then refresh in ice water to stop the cooking and to preserve its color. Drain and cut into 2-inch pieces.

3 Combine the noodles, asparagus, carrots, onion, and red pepper together in a large bowl.

4 Prepare the dressing by mixing together the shallot, soy sauce, sesame oil, rice vinegar, ginger, and honey. Stir, then pour in the grapeseed oil, whisking while pouring. Season to taste with salt and pepper.

5 Pour the dressing over the noodles, add the sesame seeds, and toss. Garnish with the cilantro.

NOTE

The easiest way to grate ginger is to peel it, place it into a resealable bag, and freeze. When a recipe calls for grated ginger, grate the frozen piece of ginger with a fine rasp grater. It becomes a soft, beautiful powder that dissolves in sauces and marinades almost instantly.

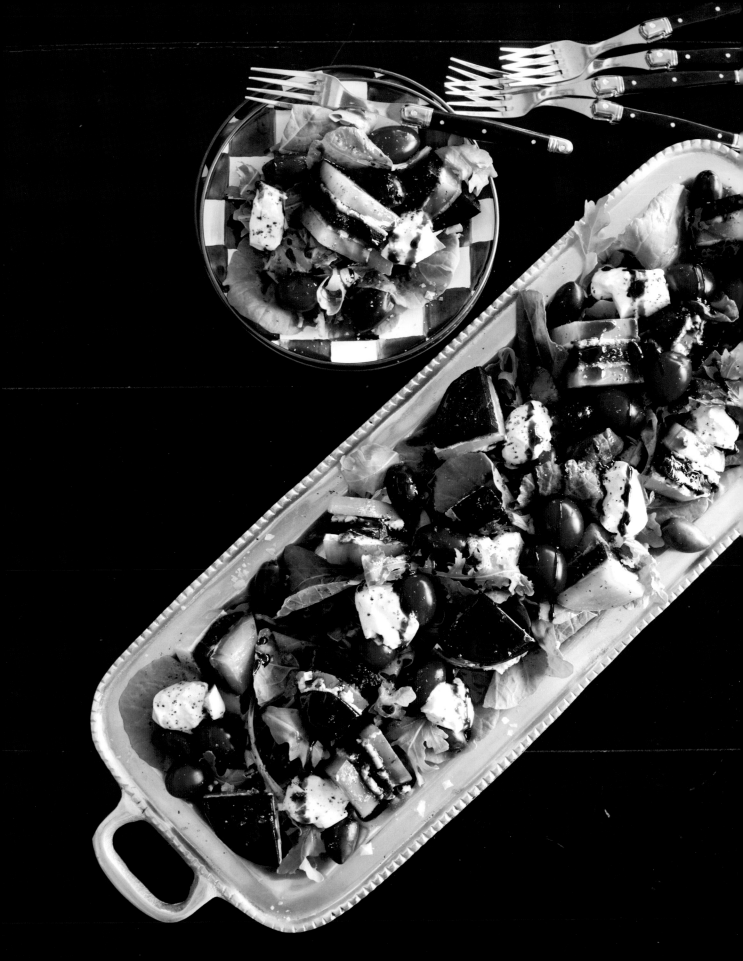

Layered Beet Salad with Burrata

Mozzarella has come a long way from the bland, rubbery shreds used on mediocre pizza. The real Italian version uses buffalo milk. Burrata is made by stretching out a thin layer of delectable mozzarella and filling it with cream. Nothing can truly define the over-the-top taste, texture, and culinary experience that burrata delivers. It has a short shelf life (3 to 4 days), so purchase according to use.

---

1 Cut the cooked and cooled beets into ¼-inch slices. Alternating colors, spread the slices with a good smear of Boursin cheese and create stacks of 3 to 5 slices. Cut each stack into quarters, and set aside.

2 Line the serving plate (or plates, for individual portions) with greens. Arrange the beet wedges on top, then scatter with the tomatoes and olives. Cut the burrata into walnut-sized chunks and scatter them evenly over the salad. Drizzle with extra virgin olive oil and an artsy squeeze of the Balsamic Glaze. A little fleur de sel and a good grinding of pepper finish the salad perfectly.

INGREDIENTS

2 large red beets, peeled, boiled, drained, and cooled (see note)

2 large yellow beets, peeled, boiled, drained, and cooled (see note)

1 package (5.2 oz) Boursin cheese, original flavor

3 cups arugula or mâche leaves (see note)

20 grape tomatoes

20 pitted kalamata olives

1 ½ balls (12 oz) burrata cheese (see note, page 90)

Extra virgin olive oil, for drizzling

Balsamic Glaze, for drizzling (page 168; or use store-bought)

Fleur de sel and freshly ground pepper

SERVES 6

NOTES

The easiest way to prepare beets is to peel them raw. They bleed less in their raw state than when they are cooked. I peel, boil, drain, and cool in that order. Depending on the size of the beets, I usually boil them for about 20 minutes.

Mâche, or lamb's lettuce as it is sometimes called, is a delicate soft leaf the size of a loonie. It is French in origin and unfortunately not that easy to access unless you grow it yourself. Specialty stores have it but don't knock yourself out trying to find it. Arugula is just fine.

Beet, Orange, and Fennel Salad

INGREDIENTS

2 large red beets, peeled,
   boiled, drained, and
   cooled (see note, page 97)
1 medium bulb fresh fennel
3 medium navel oranges
½ cup finely sliced red onion
12 pitted kalamata olives,
   quartered
½ cup chopped fresh mint
   leaves (garnish)
⅓ cup chopped toasted
   pistachio nuts (optional
   garnish; see page 166)
Fleur de sel and freshly
   ground pepper

DRESSING

2 Tbsp Dijon mustard
¼ cup blood orange vinegar
   (see note)
⅔ cup extra virgin olive oil
Fleur de sel and freshly
   ground pepper

SERVES 6 TO 8

The crisp, bright taste of fennel, intense richness of beets, and fresh citrusy orange segments make for an amazing salad that just dances in your mouth.

———

1 For the dressing, place the mustard in a small bowl, add the vinegar, and slowly whisk in the oil. Season with fleur de sel and freshly ground pepper to taste. Set aside.

2 When the beets are cool enough to handle, chop them in half, then thinly slice and set aside.

3 Cut the fennel in half and remove the woody core. Carefully slice the fennel using a mandoline or, for slightly thicker slices, use a sharp knife. Set aside.

4 Peel the oranges, then carefully cut down either side of each segment to eliminate the connective membrane. Repeat with the remaining oranges.

5 To assemble, choose a large oval serving tray and lay the fennel on one side of the tray. Lay the sliced beets on the opposite side of the tray, overlapping in an attractive pattern and leaving a space down the center of the tray. Heap the segmented oranges down the center. Evenly scatter the red onion over top of the whole salad and sprinkle the olives on top. Drizzle the dressing over top and garnish with the mint and pistachio nuts, if using. Sprinkle with a few good pinches of fleur de sel and a good grinding of pepper.

NOTE
Fruit vinegars in a variety of flavors are finding their way into salad dressings more and more. They are quite common and easy to find in gourmet stores or online. If you cannot source blood orange vinegar, substitute the same amount of white balsamic (see page 4) plus 2 teaspoons of orange zest.

The Wedge with Roasted Garlic Parmesan Dressing and Pancetta Soldiers

I know the wedge is rather old-school—a steakhouse salad that has never been crowned with anything other than a thick blue cheese or ranch dressing. But a wedge salad can be refreshingly crisp and delicious. It just needs an update, so here it is.

———

1 Preheat your oven to 325°F.

2 To make the dressing, cut ¼ inch off the top of the garlic, drizzle with the olive oil, wrap loosely in foil, and bake for about 45 to 60 minutes, or until the garlic is soft and light golden brown. Remove and cool. Adjust the oven to 350°F.

3 Place the buttermilk, Parmesan cheese, mayonnaise, sour cream, shallot, and pepper in a bowl. Whisk to combine. Peel the roasted garlic, place the cloves in a small bowl, and squish them with the back of a spoon. Add the squished garlic to the dressing bowl and whisk in until the dressing is smooth. Season with salt according to taste and set aside.

4 For the pancetta soldiers, line one baking sheet with parchment. Lay the pancetta slices on the parchment and top with another piece of parchment. Place the other baking sheet on top and bake for about 20 minutes. Remove and cool. Lift off the baking sheet and parchment and transfer the pancetta soldiers to a few sheets of paper towel to absorb any excess fat. Set aside.

5 Cut the lettuce head in half, then cut each half in thirds. Place each wedge on a salad plate, cut two slits into each wedge, and slide one of the pancetta soldiers into each slit; you will have two soldiers per wedge.

6 Drizzle the dressing over the wedges and serve.

INGREDIENTS
12 slices Italian pancetta
1 large head iceberg lettuce

DRESSING
1 whole head garlic
1 tsp extra virgin olive oil
1 cup buttermilk
½ cup freshly grated
    Parmesan cheese
¼ cup mayonnaise
¼ cup sour cream
1 small shallot, finely minced
1 tsp freshly ground pepper
Sea salt

SPECIAL EQUIPMENT
2 baking sheets of the
    same size

SERVES 6

Farro Salad with Charred Broccoli

INGREDIENTS

2 cups farro

2 lb broccoli, trimmed and
    cut into florets

2 Tbsp extra virgin olive oil

Fleur de sel

½ lemon, for squeezing

⅔ cup Pesto (page 170; or
    use store-bought)

1 cup chopped sun-dried
    tomatoes

½ cup toasted pine nuts or
    almonds (see page 166)

½ cup finely chopped fresh
    Italian parsley

Freshly ground pepper

⅓ cup freshly grated
    Parmesan cheese
    (garnish)

SERVES 6 TO 8

Farro, or emmer, is an ancient grain that has a chewy texture and rather nutty flavor. It is high in fiber and protein, making it a runaway pick in healthy eating. I combine it with charred broccoli to bring it into the modern culinary world. This salad is a perfect choice for lunch or as a side for any main.

———

1 Rinse and drain the farro, transfer to a saucepan, and add 4 cups of water. Cover and bring to a boil, then turn down to a simmer for about 40 minutes, or until the liquid is absorbed and the farro is tender and cooked. Drain off any excess water and let cool.

2 While the farro is cooling, heat your barbecue or grill pan to medium-high. Lightly toss the broccoli with the olive oil and char on all sides for about 20 minutes, turning occasionally; you want the broccoli blackened all over. Season with a bit of fleur de sel while it is cooking. Once the broccoli florets are all charred, transfer to a bowl and give them a good squeeze of lemon juice.

3 To serve, place the farro in a serving dish, spoon the pesto over, and mix well to distribute evenly. Add the sun-dried tomatoes, nuts, parsley, and charred broccoli.

4 Taste for seasoning and give it a grind of fresh pepper if you like. Finish with the Parmesan cheese.

NOTE
The blood orange oil can be subbed with the same quantity
of olive oil and 1 extra teaspoon of orange zest.

Wild and Forbidden Rice Salad

Wild rice is not really rice at all, but a grain. I think this gorgeous gift from the center of Canada is underappreciated and not served frequently enough. Pairing it with forbidden rice makes for a delicious salad.

---

1 In a pot, cook the wild rice in 5 cups of water; do not add any salt. Bring to a boil, then cover, lower the heat, and simmer until the rice puffs open, revealing a white center, and is soft to eat. This will take about 45 minutes. If the liquid runs out before the rice is cooked, just add more water, ½ cup at a time. You can always drain off any excess water later.

2 At the same time, cook the forbidden rice by placing the rice and 2 cups of water in a pot. Bring to a boil, then cover, lower the heat and simmer until cooked through, about 15 to 18 minutes.

3 Drain any remaining water from the wild rice in a colander and set both types of rice aside to cool.

4 Heat the sherry or port wine in a small pot over medium-low heat, add the figs, turn off the heat, and let the figs sit until they absorb most of the liquid. This will take about 15 minutes.

5 Place both types of rice in a large shallow bowl, add the blood orange oil and the olive oil, and toss through. Add the shallot, orange zest, orange juice, soaked figs, and any sherry left in the pot to the rice mixture.

6 Mix well to distribute all the ingredients, then add the mint and season to taste with salt and pepper. This salad is best made at least 3 hours before serving, or the day before. Chill until ready to serve. Just before serving, sprinkle the toasted pecans and julienned orange zest over top.

INGREDIENTS

1½ cups wild rice

1 cup forbidden rice (see recipe introduction, page 44)

⅓ cup sweet sherry or port wine

1 cup chopped dried figs

¼ cup blood orange oil (I like O Blood Orange Olive Oil; see note)

¼ cup extra virgin olive oil

1 medium shallot, finely minced

Zest of 1 small orange

⅓ cup fresh orange juice

⅓ cup finely chopped fresh mint

Sea salt and freshly ground pepper

1 cup chopped toasted pecans (see page 166)

Julienned orange zest (garnish)

SERVES 6 TO 8

Brian's Shredded Vegetable Salad

INGREDIENTS

Kosher salt

1 heaping cup frozen shelled
   edamame beans

1 heaping cup finely
   shredded napa cabbage

1 heaping cup finely
   shredded kale leaves

1 cup julienned jicama (see
   note, page 89)

3 Lebanese cucumbers,
   julienned (see note)

2 medium carrots, grated

12 snow peas, strings
   removed and julienned

12 radishes, finely sliced

I created this salad for my friend Brian. He is a super-healthy cyclist who turns his nose up at all things that are creamy, cheesy, or, as he says, "shputzy." This super salad is all about crunch, texture, fiber, and health. This one is for you, my friend!

1 Fill a medium pot with water and bring to a boil. Once boiling, salt the water and blanch the edamame beans for 3 to 4 minutes. Drain and immediately transfer to a large bowl of ice water to stop the cooking process and to preserve their color. Once cooled, drain well and set aside.

2 Prepare the rest of the vegetables and herbs and toss together with the edamame in a large bowl.

3 For the dressing, combine the garlic, shallot, soy sauce, yuzu vinegar, mustard, sesame oil, ginger, and chili paste. Slowly pour in the grapeseed oil, whisking the whole time, until the dressing comes together. Season to taste with salt and pepper.

4 Pour the dressing over the salad, toss well to coat, and garnish with the toasted almonds.

NOTES

Small Lebanese cucumbers are available at many grocers. If these are unavailable, you can quarter and julienne an English cucumber instead. One long English cucumber equals roughly 3 to 4 mini Lebanese cucumbers.

Yuzu is a Japanese citrus fruit. The vinegar can be purchased at good gourmet stores and keeps well for months. If it is not available, substitute the same amount of white balsamic (see page 4) plus a squeeze of fresh lime juice.

---

10 to 12 yellow grape tomatoes, halved

2 big handfuls arugula

½ cup chopped fresh cilantro

½ cup chopped fresh basil

½ cup chopped fresh mint

1 cup chopped toasted almonds (garnish; see page 166)

DRESSING

2 cloves garlic, minced

1 large shallot, finely minced

2 Tbsp soy sauce

2 Tbsp yuzu vinegar (see note)

1 heaping Tbsp Dijon mustard

1 Tbsp toasted sesame oil (see page 5)

2 tsp grated ginger (see note, page 94)

1 tsp chili paste (see page 4)

½ cup roasted grapeseed oil

Sea salt and freshly ground pepper

SERVES 6 TO 8

Deconstructed Classic American Cobb Salad

Cobb salad is my ultimate favorite summer salad. It is hugely popular in the US, and whenever I visit, it is my go-to lunch. The Cobb has it all: chicken, bacon, avocado, egg, and blue cheese. I have chosen to do this salad in a deconstructed format to be a bit different.

---

1 For the dressing, place the vinegar, mustard, and garlic in a small bowl, then whisk in the olive oil and honey and add the salt and pepper to taste. Set aside.

2 In a high-sided sauté pan over low heat, heat the chicken stock to a simmer, add the chicken breasts, and let them poach in the stock for about 10 minutes, or until the chicken is cooked completely through. Remove and let the chicken cool on a plate. Once it is cool, shred or cut into ½-inch cubes.

3 To prepare the salad, line a platter (I use a 14-inch square platter) with the lettuce. Arrange the remaining ingredients tightly in rows across the lettuce. Serve the dressing on the side.

NOTES

For a creamy dressing, simply add ½ cup of sour cream or mayonnaise to the prepared dressing.

I like to spray my measuring spoon with cooking oil before measuring honey; it allows the honey to just glide off the spoon.

INGREDIENTS

2 cups chicken stock

2 boneless, skinless chicken breasts

1 large head iceberg lettuce, coarsely chopped

12 thin slices bacon, fried crisp and crumbled

2 cups grape tomatoes, halved

6 oz blue cheese, crumbled, such as Stilton, Roquefort, or Blue Moon

3 large free-range eggs, hard-boiled, peeled, and quartered

2 avocados, diced

DRESSING

2 Tbsp good-quality aged red wine vinegar

1 Tbsp Dijon mustard

1 clove garlic, minced

⅔ cup extra virgin olive oil

1 tsp liquid honey (see note)

Sea salt and freshly ground pepper

SERVES 6 TO 8

Diane's Endive, Radicchio, and Globe Grape Salad

INGREDIENTS

1 head Belgian endive

½ small head radicchio

3 heaping cups spring
   salad mix

½ cup halved and seeded
   red globe grapes (see
   note)

½ cup fresh Parmesan
   cheese shavings
   (garnish)

DRESSING

⅓ cup extra virgin olive oil

1 Tbsp white balsamic
   vinegar (see page 4)

1 Tbsp pure Canadian maple
   syrup

2 tsp Dijon mustard

Fleur de sel and freshly
   ground pepper

SERVES 4

My bestie from high school, Diane Lawrence, is one of the best bakers I have ever met, and her savory culinary creations are pretty darn good as well. Because desserts aren't featured in this book, I asked for her favorite hip salad, and here is her contribution. We have come a long way from home economics at Templeton High, my friend.

––––––––––––

1 Tear the endive leaves in half and place in a bowl. Tear the radicchio leaves in half and add to the bowl. Add the salad mix and the grapes. Chill and set aside until ready to serve.

2 For the dressing, place the olive oil, balsamic, maple syrup, and mustard in a 1-cup screw-top jar, and shake vigorously until the dressing is combined. Season with fleur de sel and pepper to taste.

3 When you are ready to serve, pour half the dressing over the salad mixture and toss to coat. If you need more, add a little at a time so as not to overdress.

4 Divide evenly among four salad plates and garnish with the Parmesan shavings.

NOTE

If you are unable to find red globe grapes, use large red grapes instead.

Heirloom Tomatoes with Herbed Ricotta

There was a time when ricotta was reserved for ripple-edged lasagna. Today, ricotta is one of the most inspired cheeses to make yourself, but it is also readily available at most supermarkets, delis, and gourmet markets. A tomato is considered heirloom if its seeds have been passed down through generations because of their special characteristics. They are worth seeking out in farmers' markets, where they are in abundance. Don't be discouraged by blemishes and radical shapes; this is to be expected from honestly grown organic heirlooms.

---

1 To make the herbed ricotta, mix together the ricotta, parsley, basil, tarragon, mint, and lemon zest in a bowl. Stir well to combine. Cover and chill until ready to use; this can be made in advance and will keep in the fridge for 3 to 4 days.

2 To make the dressing, mix together the olive oil, lemon juice, and pomegranate molasses.

3 To serve, slice the tomatoes and lay them on a platter. Drizzle the dressing evenly over the tomatoes and sprinkle with the toasted nuts. Using a teaspoon, randomly scatter the prepared ricotta all over the dish.

4 Finish with fleur de sel and a good grinding of fresh pepper to taste, and serve.

INGREDIENTS

2 cups fresh ricotta
⅓ cup chopped fresh parsley
⅓ cup chopped fresh basil
⅓ cup chopped fresh tarragon
⅓ cup chopped fresh mint
1 tsp fresh lemon zest
2 lb mixed varietal heirloom tomatoes
⅔ cup toasted pine nuts, or any toasted nut of your choice (see page 166)
Fleur de sel and freshly ground pepper

DRESSING

½ cup extra virgin olive oil
2 Tbsp fresh lemon juice
1 Tbsp pomegranate molasses (see note)

SERVES 6

NOTE
Pomegranate molasses is an essential ingredient in Middle Eastern cooking. It is simply a reduction of pomegranate juice and sugar. You can substitute equal parts balsamic and honey if you cannot find the molasses.

Kale Caesar

INGREDIENTS

1 cup raw pumpkin seeds

1 Tbsp chili oil

1 bunch kale, stemmed and
ribs removed

1 head Treviso radicchio (see
note)

½ cup chopped fresh Italian
parsley leaves

½ cup fresh basil chiffonade
(see note, page 66)

½ cup grated Asiago cheese
(garnish)

DRESSING

4 anchovy fillets

1 free-range egg yolk

Juice of ½ small lemon

1 Tbsp Dijon mustard

2 cloves garlic, minced

1 tsp Worcestershire sauce

½ tsp freshly ground pepper

½ cup extra virgin olive oil

SERVES 6 TO 8

Even though the kale obsession is somewhat fading, the health aspect is still real. Globally, Caesar salad is still one of the most ordered salads in restaurants. This version is certainly worth trying for all of you kale lovers out there.

1 Preheat your oven to 300°F.

2 For the dressing, place the anchovies, egg yolk, lemon juice, mustard, garlic, Worcestershire sauce, and pepper into the bowl of a food processor fitted with the metal blade. Pulse a few times, stopping to scrape down the sides of the bowl. With the machine running, slowly pour in the olive oil in a steady stream. The dressing will become smooth and creamy. Adjust the seasoning to suit your taste. Set aside.

3 Place the pumpkin seeds in a bowl, pour the chili oil over top, and toss well so that the seeds are lightly dressed with oil. Transfer to a small baking sheet and roast for about 15 minutes, or until golden brown. Remove, cool, and set aside.

4 To prepare the salad, stack the kale leaves on top of each other, about three leaves thick. Roll them up tight like a cigar and chop into ¼-inch pieces. Repeat until the whole bunch is chopped. Place in a large bowl. Cut the radicchio in half lengthwise, remove the small core at the bottom, and lay the cut side flat on your counter. Cut into pieces the same size as the kale and add them to the bowl along with the parsley and basil. The salad greens can be prepared to this point up to 3 hours ahead and kept in the refrigerator.

5 When ready to serve, toss the greens together, then pour a small portion of the dressing over top, tossing to coat all the leaves evenly. Do not overdress. You will have leftover dressing for sure, so be careful not to overdo it. The dressing will keep in the refrigerator for up to 5 days.

6 Transfer the salad to your serving bowl and garnish with the toasted pumpkin seeds and grated Asiago.

NOTE
Treviso is a milder variety of Italian radicchio. Its elongated shape is quite different than its cousin's classic round, compact ball. Use regular radicchio if Treviso is unavailable.

Rice Salad in a Jar

Salad in a jar? Really. It is the cute presentation and the gorgeous layered colors that provoke lively conversation for this salad course. It can be made hours ahead, chilled, and served on a buffet table, or presented in the jars on small dishes for an individual plating.

───────────

1 Place the rice and 2 cups of water in a saucepan. Cover and bring to a boil, then turn the heat down to a simmer until the rice is cooked through and all the water is absorbed, about 15 to 18 minutes.

2 While the rice is cooking, prepare the dressing. In a small bowl, mix together the garlic, shallot, vinegar, and mustard. Slowly whisk in both oils, season with fleur de sel and pepper to taste, and set aside.

3 Once the rice is cooked, fluff it a little with a fork, then pour the dressing over the hot rice. Set aside and let the rice cool. Once the rice is cool, you can begin the assembly.

4 Start by cutting the peppers into 1-inch pieces, and lay a piece in the bottom of each jar. Top with a heaping soupspoon of rice, then add a few cubes of avocado, some bocconcini, and some of the shredded basil. Top with another soupspoon of rice and repeat the layers.

5 Chill until serving. Just before serving, sprinkle with the toasted nuts. Do not add nuts ahead of time, as they will become soft.

NOTE
Feel free to substitute ingredients or add in your personal favorites, like pitted kalamata olives, sun-dried tomatoes, grape tomatoes, and/or chopped artichokes.

INGREDIENTS

1 cup forbidden rice (see recipe introduction, page 44)

1 jar (6 oz) roasted red peppers, drained and blotted dry on paper towel

1 avocado, diced into ½-inch cubes

⅔ cup pearl bocconcini (see note, page 59)

6 large fresh basil leaves, cut into chiffonade (see note, page 66)

½ cup chopped toasted almonds or any nut of your choice (see page 166)

DRESSING

1 small clove garlic, minced

1 small shallot, finely minced

2 Tbsp balsamic vinegar

1 Tbsp Dijon mustard

⅓ cup extra virgin olive oil

¼ cup lemon-infused extra virgin olive oil (see note, page 87)

Fleur de sel and freshly ground pepper

SPECIAL EQUIPMENT

Six 7 or 8 oz Mason jars or any preserving jars

SERVES 6

Shaved Fennel and Bresaola Salad

INGREDIENTS

1 medium bulb fresh fennel

6 oz thinly sliced bresaola
   (see note)

1 cup fresh Parmesan
   cheese shavings

½ cup whole fresh Italian
   parsley leaves

⅓ cup Crispy Capers
   (page 168)

Fleur de sel and freshly
   ground pepper

DRESSING

Juice of ½ lemon

2 to 3 tsp truffle oil

SERVES 6

The licorice essence of freshly shaved fennel combined with thinly sliced bresaola is rather magical. Crispy Capers and shaved Parmesan top this dish off perfectly.

———

1 For the dressing, mix the lemon juice and truffle oil together to taste, then set aside.

2 Cut the fennel bulb in half and remove the woody core. Carefully slice the fennel using a mandoline or, for slightly thicker slices, use a sharp knife. Arrange the fennel slices in a single layer on your serving platter (see note).

3 Pinch each bresaola slice in the middle to form a flower shape. Randomly place these all over the sliced fennel.

4 Drizzle with the dressing, then top with the Parmesan shavings, parsley leaves, and capers. Finish with fleur de sel and a good grinding of pepper to suit your taste.

NOTES

Bresaola is air-dried beef and can be found at Italian delis.

This salad looks great served on a round platter.

Layered Niçoise Salad

INGREDIENTS

1 ½ lb fresh tuna

Sea salt and freshly ground
pepper

½ cup black sesame seeds

½ cup white sesame seeds

Roasted grapeseed oil, for
grilling or frying

3 cups mixed greens

1 lb small Yukon gold or
purple Peruvian potatoes
(see note, page 80),
boiled and sliced

Not all Niçoise salads are created equal. Using fresh tuna as opposed to the canned option elevates this salad to new heights. I like to serve it in a glass dish so you can see all the bright colors. This is a perfect salad for a summer buffet, or a gorgeous potluck dish.

---

1 To make the dressing, place the shallots, garlic, rice vinegar, tequila (if using), soy sauce, sesame oil, and wasabi powder to taste in a medium bowl. Whisk together to combine. In a slow, steady stream, pour in the grapeseed oil, whisking while you pour, until the dressing is smooth and creamy. Season with fleur de sel and pepper to taste, and set aside.

2 Season the tuna with sea salt and pepper. Mix both sesame seeds together and coat both sides of the tuna with seeds, shaking off the excess.

3 Heat your grill or fry pan to high and brush it lightly with grapeseed oil. Sear the tuna on both sides, about 2 minutes each, depending on how well done you like your tuna. Remove and set aside to cool. Once the tuna is cool enough to handle, break it into chunks.

4 In your serving bowl, begin the layering process with the greens on the bottom, then the sliced potatoes, green beans, grape tomatoes, onion, eggs, pepper, olives, and tuna. Finish with a sprinkling of finely chopped parsley and julienned lemon zest. Drizzle the dressing all over, and serve.

NOTE

You can find wasabi powder at many gourmet or Japanese stores. It is generally combined with water to create a paste, but here I have stirred it into the dressing for a bit of a kick.

---

1 lb green beans, steamed and refreshed in ice water

2 cups grape tomatoes, halved

1 medium sweet onion, thinly sliced

3 large free-range eggs, hard-boiled, peeled, and sliced

1 medium yellow pepper, julienned

1 cup pitted Niçoise olives (these are the tiny French variety)

⅓ cup finely chopped fresh parsley (garnish)

Julienned lemon zest (garnish)

DRESSING

2 small shallots, finely minced

1 large clove garlic, minced

2 Tbsp rice vinegar

2 Tbsp tequila (optional)

1 Tbsp soy sauce

2 tsp toasted sesame oil (see page 5)

1 to 2 tsp wasabi powder (see note)

⅔ cup roasted grapeseed oil

Fleur de sel and freshly ground pepper

SERVES 6 TO 8

Counterclockwise from top: Penne Arrabbiata My Way
(page 161); Angel Hair Pasta with Grape Tomatoes
(page 160); Spaghetti Carbonara (page 157)

Sexy Sides

Boiled potatoes, steamed broccoli, or canned creamed corn do not constitute a sexy side in any way. Sexy sides have layered textures, riots of flavor, color, and creativity, and they demand second helpings!

Sides are an incredibly important part of your meal: they can create variety and add interest to any dinner. Let's be honest, we all know what chicken and roast beef taste like. The seasoning and prep may change from chef to chef, but it is only with your side dishes that a meal can really be transformed. I want the side dishes to your dinners to play a major role. Close your eyes and think of jacket roasted sweet potatoes crowned with herbed feta and crispy chorizo, and you will start to picture what I am talking about . . .

It doesn't have to be complicated. I am talking about giving something as simple as cauliflower a brand new look and taste. Sliced into thick steaks and then panfried with salty capers and tart lemon, it becomes glistening golden brown and crisp. On page 134, broccolini is charred until smoky and then made sexy by tossing it into a magical miso dressing and finishing with garlic chips. It's about getting out of the rut—changing up button mushrooms for the new kid on the block, shimeji, or opting for black forbidden rice instead of pedestrian white. These simple yet surprising combinations will reinvent the dishes you think you already know. These kinds of flavors and combinations are usually only found in trendy restaurants, but now you can create them at home. So put away your done and done standby dishes; get your sexy on, and let's cook!

Green Beans 2.0

INGREDIENTS

2 Tbsp roasted grapeseed or
  peanut oil
1 lb skinny green beans
  (haricots verts), washed
  and trimmed
4 Tbsp soy sauce
4 Tbsp chili paste (see page 4)
2 Tbsp grated ginger (see
  note, page 94)
3 cloves garlic, minced
⅓ cup toasted sesame
  seeds (garnish)

SERVES 6

The skinny French green beans called haricots verts are perfect for this dish and are readily available at good produce stores. The spicy, salty, and savory combination of soy sauce, ginger, garlic, and chili turns this dish of simple green beans into a sexy side. You can alternatively use broccolini, asparagus, or portobello mushrooms in place of the beans. Step back and take the accolades!

---

1 Heat a nonstick fry pan to high heat, add the oil, and swirl to coat. Add the beans and shake until they begin to crackle and brown. Continue to sauté on medium-high heat for 5 minutes, shaking occasionally.

2 Mix together the soy sauce, chili paste, ginger, and garlic, and pour over the hot beans in the pan. Sauté on medium-high for 1 minute.

3 Transfer to a serving platter and garnish generously with the sesame seeds.

Fragrant Basmati Rice

This easy-to-prepare rice side dish complements most mains, especially chicken, lamb, or fish. It is important to give the rice a good wash to remove excess starch, which causes the rice to clump together. At least two to three washes are necessary before the water runs clear.

INGREDIENTS

2 cups basmati rice

2 Tbsp unsalted butter

1 small onion, finely diced

4-inch cinnamon stick

4 whole star anise

6 whole cloves

3 green cardamom pods,
   lightly crushed

1 tsp ground turmeric

Two 4-inch strips orange zest

Pinch of sea salt

SERVES 6

1 Wash the rice in a bowl of cold water, rinse, and repeat until the water is clear. Drain and set aside.

2 In a pot over medium heat, melt the butter, add the onion, and sauté until the onion begins to soften, about 5 minutes. Add the cinnamon, star anise, cloves, cardamom, and turmeric, give it a good stir, and cover. Keep the heat on low until the onion is soft, about 5 to 7 minutes.

3 Add the rice to the pot along with 4 cups of water, 1 strip of orange zest, and the pinch of sea salt. Bring to a boil, then cover and turn down to a simmer. Continue to simmer until the water is absorbed and the rice is cooked, about 15 to 20 minutes.

4 Transfer to a serving bowl and garnish with the spices from the rice and the remaining strip of orange zest.

Cauliflower Steaks with Capers and Caramelized Lemon

INGREDIENTS

1 large head cauliflower,
    trimmed of all leaves
⅓ cup extra virgin olive oil
½ cup capers, drained and
    blotted dry
1 lemon, cut into 6 wedges
Fleur de sel and freshly
    ground pepper

SERVES 6

Forget the steamed florets; bring on steak-thick slices of this newly celebrated vegetable and layer them with lemons and capers. This is new-wave cauliflower at its best! It marries well with fish and is a great holiday side.

---

1 Hold the cauliflower firmly on your cutting board and slice into ½-inch slices. The first slice or two will be a bit awkward, but then it becomes easy. Do not remove the core; this is what keeps each slice together.

2 In 2 large nonstick fry pans, heat the oil on medium-high. Divide the cauliflower slices between the pans and let them sizzle away for about 8 to 10 minutes. Using a spatula, carefully lift and flip, being careful not to break them. If you find the large slices are too difficult to maneuver, cut them in half.

3 After flipping the cauliflower slices, add the capers and lemon wedges to the pans. Continue to sauté until the cauliflower and lemon wedges are golden brown. Remove the cauliflower and capers to a serving platter, and squeeze the warm lemon on top, leaving the wedges on the plate for a rustic presentation if desired. Finish with a few good pinches of fleur de sel and generous grindings of pepper. Serve hot. It is hard to hold yourself back.

NOTE
You can also fry this in two batches, dividing the total amount of capers and lemon wedges between the batches. Simply keep the first batch warm in the oven at 375°F while frying the second.

Rutabaga with Crispy Shallots

INGREDIENTS

4 large shallots, thinly sliced

1 Tbsp unbleached all-
purpose flour

4 Tbsp roasted grapeseed oil

2 medium rutabagas, peeled
and cubed

1 medium russet potato,
peeled and cubed

1 small carrot, peeled and
cubed

Kosher salt

⅓ cup whipping cream
(33%)

⅓ cup unsalted butter

Sea salt and freshly ground
pepper

SERVES 6

In all honesty, my least favorite foods have always been turnips (rutabagas), parsnips, and pretty much any strong-flavored vegetable such as Brussels sprouts. But, with the addition of crispy shallots, this rutabaga dish is a revelation in taste and composition. Turnips take on a new taste.

---

1 Place the shallots and flour in a clean plastic produce bag, twist the top, and shake vigorously to coat the shallots in the flour. Transfer to a sieve and shake out any excess flour.

2 Heat a nonstick fry pan on medium-low heat, and add the grapeseed oil and the floured shallots. While frying, stir the shallots and shake the pan occasionally to encourage even browning. Fry until they are all golden brown and crisp, about 15 to 20 minutes. Remove with a slotted spoon and transfer to a paper-towel-lined plate to absorb any excess oil. Set aside.

3 In a large pot, place the rutabagas, potato, and carrot, and fill with just enough water to cover the vegetables. Salt the water, bring to a boil, then lower the heat and simmer until they are cooked through and soft, about 15 to 18 minutes. Drain and let the steam subside, then transfer to the bowl of a food processor. Add the cream and butter and purée until smooth.

4 Transfer the purée to a serving vessel, fold in the reserved shallots, and season with salt and pepper. Serve hot.

Not-So-Green Fried Tomatoes

Summer produces a bounty of produce, and heirloom toma-toes are one of those tasty luxuries. When you can't wait for the ripening of the Green Zebra (an heirloom variety), follow the movie and fry.

———

1 Slice the tomatoes into ½-inch slices and lay them in a single layer on a plate. Sprinkle with the kosher salt and let them sit for about 15 minutes to release some of their moisture.

2 Mix the cornmeal, flour, cheese, and paprika together and set aside. Place the buttermilk in a separate dish and set aside. Heat a nonstick fry pan on medium-high, and add the grapeseed oil.

3 Blot the tomato slices with paper towel to remove the moisture, dip them into the buttermilk, and then generously coat with the cornmeal mixture. Working in batches, fry them on both sides in the hot pan until golden brown, about 5 min-utes per side. Remove to a paper-towel-lined plate and blot once again with paper towel to remove excess oil.

4 Place on a serving plate and sprinkle with fleur de sel and ground pepper to taste. Mix the sour cream together with the pesto and serve with the fried tomatoes. Serve warm.

INGREDIENTS

4 unripe Green Zebra tomatoes (see note)

2 tsp kosher salt

½ cup cornmeal

½ cup unbleached all-purpose flour

½ cup freshly grated Romano or Parmesan cheese

2 tsp sweet or hot smoked Spanish paprika (see page 5)

½ cup buttermilk

⅓ cup roasted grapeseed oil

Fleur de sel and freshly ground pepper

½ cup sour cream

½ cup Pesto (page 170; or use store-bought)

SERVES 4 TO 6

NOTE
If you can't find Green Zebras, you can use any other variety of green tomato. If, however, green tomatoes are not available, sub in firm red romas or firm yellow tomatoes, as pictured.

Roasted Butternut Squash and Fried Halloumi

INGREDIENTS

1 butternut squash (about
    2 lb), peeled and cut into
    1-inch cubes

1 large red onion, cut into
    1-inch pieces

⅓ cup plus 2 Tbsp roasted
    grapeseed oil

⅓ cup dukkah (see note,
    page 31) or Moroccan
    seasoning spice blend

¼ cup unbleached all-
    purpose flour

9 oz halloumi cheese, cut
    into 1-inch cubes (see
    note, page 56)

⅓ cup finely chopped fresh
    Italian parsley

½ cup chopped toasted
    hazelnuts (garnish; see
    page 166)

Freshly ground pepper

DRESSING

1 cup plain Greek yogurt
¼ cup sour cream
1 tsp chili flakes
1 tsp fresh lemon zest
2 tsp fresh lemon juice
Kosher salt

SERVES 6

Dredging butternut squash cubes in dukkah or Moroccan spice blend and roasting them until golden brown does two things: it gives a kick to an otherwise bland vegetable, and it provides a nice crust. A refreshing lemon Greek yogurt dressing with crisp cubes of halloumi round this off nicely, while toasted hazelnuts provide the finishing crunch.

---

1 Preheat your oven to 400°F.

2 To make the dressing, in a bowl, combine the yogurt, sour cream, chili flakes, lemon zest and juice, and kosher salt to taste. Stir well. Cover and chill until ready to serve.

3 Place the squash cubes and red onion in a large bowl, drizzle in ⅓ cup grapeseed oil, and toss well to ensure that each piece is kissed with the oil. Sprinkle in the dukkah or spice blend and toss well to coat. Transfer to a roasting pan or parchment-lined cookie sheet, ensuring that the vegetables are spread in a single layer and not heaped. Roast in the oven for about 40 minutes, or until golden brown. Turn the squash and onion once or twice to encourage even browning.

4 About 10 minutes before the vegetables are finished roasting, place the flour in a bowl, add the halloumi cubes, and toss to coat evenly with the flour. Tip into a fine sieve and shake to remove any excess flour.

5 Heat a nonstick fry pan on medium-high heat, add the remaining oil, and fry the cheese on all sides until golden brown, about 3 to 5 minutes. Work in batches if necessary so as not to crowd the pan. Transfer to a paper-towel-lined plate to absorb any excess oil.

6 To serve, transfer the squash mixture to a serving platter. Scatter the crisp halloumi over top, then the chopped parsley. Finish with a grinding of pepper. Garnish with hazelnuts and serve warm or at room temperature with the dressing on the side.

NOTE
This can easily double as a salad. Simply line your plate with spinach leaves and top with the squash and halloumi.

Charred Miso Broccolini with Crispy Garlic Chips

INGREDIENTS

Kosher salt

2 lb broccolini or broccoli
    florets

2 Tbsp roasted grapeseed oil

2 Tbsp mirin

2 Tbsp white miso paste

1 Tbsp soy sauce

2 tsp toasted sesame oil
    (see page 5)

1 tsp chili flakes (optional)

1 Tbsp extra virgin olive oil

2 large cloves garlic, thinly
    sliced

SERVES 6

The simple charring of this vegetable gives it a smoky, some-what mysterious flavor. If broccolini is not available in your area, simply sub in regular broccoli florets.

---

1 Blanch the broccolini in a large pot of boiling salted water for 2 minutes; do not overcook. Transfer to an ice water bath to refresh, then drain.

2 Toss the broccolini with 1 tablespoon of grapeseed oil so it is lightly kissed with oil; do not be tempted to add more. Heat your barbecue or grill pan to medium-high. Grill the broccolini on all sides until it becomes charred, about 10 to 15 minutes. Don't be timid to char it; this is the essence of the dish. Keep turning occasionally so each piece is evenly charred.

3 While the broccolini is charring, mix together the mirin, miso paste, soy sauce, sesame oil, the remaining grapeseed oil, and the chili flakes, if using.

4 Heat the olive oil in a small fry pan over medium-low heat and brown the garlic slices, being careful not to burn them. Transfer to a paper-towel-lined plate to absorb excess oil.

5 To serve, toss the charred broccolini with the miso dressing, ensuring that the dressing coats the broccolini evenly. Transfer to your serving platter and sprinkle the garlic chips all over. Serve hot or cold.

Whole Roasted Cauliflower

INGREDIENTS

1 large head cauliflower,
  trimmed of all leaves

½ cup freshly grated
  Parmesan cheese

4 Tbsp mayonnaise (I like
  Hellmann's)

2 Tbsp Dijon mustard

1 Tbsp finely chopped fresh
  parsley

1 clove garlic, minced

Freshly ground pepper

SERVES 4 TO 6

As cauliflower pushes kale out of the top vegetable billing, new ways to cook and serve this delicious vegetable are increasingly emerging. It is a nice change to roast the head of cauliflower whole until the crust is bubbly and browned. Just be sure not to overcook it when steaming.

1 Preheat your oven to 450°F.

2 In a pot fitted with a steamer, steam the cauliflower for about 10 to 12 minutes, or until it is almost cooked. Make sure not to oversteam, or it will be soft.

3 While the cauliflower is steaming, in a bowl, mix together the Parmesan, mayonnaise, mustard, parsley, garlic, and pepper to taste. Mix well to ensure all the ingredients are combined. Set aside.

4 Once the cauliflower is cooked al dente, remove and place in ice water to prevent it from cooking further. Drain and let it air-dry for 15 minutes. Once the moisture has evaporated, rub the Parmesan mixture all over the cauliflower and place it on a parchment-lined cookie sheet or roasting dish. The cauliflower can be prepared to this point and refrigerated until ready to cook, up to 2 days in advance. If you do refrigerate the cauliflower, make sure you take it out 2 hours ahead of serving time so the center is not cold.

5 Roast the cauliflower for 8 to 10 minutes, or until the crust begins to bubble. Turn the oven to broil and carefully broil the top until golden brown, about 1 minute—no more, or it will burn.

6 Serve immediately, quartering the head of cauliflower to make serving more manageable.

Eggplant Rolls

This is a great side for summer entertaining, as it is served at room temperature. I like things that can be done ahead to relieve any additional stress on the day of the dinner. You could sub in zucchini slices, or do a mixture of both to create interest. This also makes a great starter!

---

1 Preheat your oven to 325°F.

2 Cut the top ¼ inch off the garlic heads, rub each with 1 teaspoon oil, and wrap in foil. Bake for about 45 to 60 minutes in the oven until soft and light golden brown. Cool, peel off the papery skin, and set aside.

3 Slice the eggplants lengthwise as thin as possible. Drain the peppers, blot dry on paper towel, and set aside. Drain the artichokes, cut into quarters, blot dry on paper towel, and set aside.

4 Heat your barbecue or grill pan to medium-high heat. Brush the eggplant slices lightly with oil and season with salt and pepper. Grill for about 2 minutes on each side, or until they are golden but not overdone. You do not want any crispy burnt edges, or the eggplant will not roll. Remove from the grill, place in a single layer on your work surface, and lightly brush the tops with the balsamic glaze.

5 Slice the red peppers to the same width as the eggplant, and lay on top. Place a piece of the artichoke at one end of each eggplant slice, and roll up, enclosing the artichoke in the middle. Top each roll with a peeled garlic clove, then insert a rosemary sprig or fancy toothpick through the clove to pierce right through each roll.

6 Transfer to a platter and serve at room temperature.

INGREDIENTS

2 whole heads garlic

2 tsp extra virgin olive oil, plus more for grilling

3 Japanese eggplants

1 jar (14 oz) roasted red peppers

1 jar (8 oz) roasted artichokes

Sea salt and freshly ground pepper

½ cup Balsamic Glaze (page 168; or use store-bought)

12 to 15 fresh 3-inch sprigs rosemary, or fancy 3-inch toothpicks

MAKES 12 TO 15 ROLLS

Grilled Corn on the Cob with Smoky Lime Butter

INGREDIENTS

⅔ cup unsalted butter,
    room temperature

2 tsp fresh lime zest

1 tsp fresh lime juice

2 tsp sweet or hot smoked
    Spanish paprika (see
    page 5)

1 tsp kosher salt

6 cobs fresh corn

2 Tbsp extra virgin olive oil

1 lime, cut into 6 wedges
    (optional garnish)

SERVES 6

Forget boiling corn; that is passé. Instead, heighten the sweet flavor by low, slow grilling on your barbecue or grill pan. Fancy food magazines always display the grilled corn husks creatively tied back, and it looks lovely. That may work for magazines, but not in reality. When the corn is ready, it is sizzling hot, and either you need asbestos fingers and the skills of a surgeon to tie back the husks, or you can just keep it real. I peel the corn, rub it lightly with olive oil, and lay it on the barbecue. No burning husks to deal with, just easy-to-serve and, importantly, easy-to-eat corn.

---

1 To make the smoky lime butter, mix together the butter, lime zest and juice, paprika, and salt. Taste for seasoning and adjust to suit your preference. The smoky lime butter can be prepared in advance and frozen; it will keep for 2 to 3 months in the freezer.

2 Lay an 8- x 12-inch piece of plastic wrap on your work surface. Transfer the butter mixture to the plastic wrap. Even out the butter and, using the plastic wrap to help you, roll it up. Squeeze and twist the ends of the plastic wrap so the butter looks like a sausage in a casing, then place it in the freezer for 30 minutes to harden.

3 Meanwhile, preheat your barbecue or grill pan to medium. Peel the corn and ensure you remove all the silk. Lightly rub the cobs with the olive oil. Slowly grill for about 15 to 20 minutes, turning frequently to avoid uneven cooking. The kernels should be a deep caramel brown.

4 When the corn is cooked, remove the smoky lime butter from the freezer, unwrap it, and slice it into ¼-inch disks. Transfer the hot corn to a serving dish and top each cob with 2 to 3 butter disks. If you like, serve with lime wedges on the side.

Wild and Mixed Mushroom Sauté

INGREDIENTS

1 cup mixed dried wild
    mushrooms (cèpes,
    porcini, boletos, or
    morels)

3 Tbsp unsalted butter

2 large shallots, finely
    minced

1 leek, white part only, finely
    sliced

2 large cloves garlic, minced

1 heaping tsp chili paste
    (see page 4)

1 tsp undiluted chicken
    stock paste

5 cups sliced mixed fresh
    mushrooms (shiitake,
    chanterelle, portobello,
    shimeji, or your favorites)

⅓ cup dry white wine

¾ cup whipping cream
    (33%)

½ cup finely chopped fresh
    parsley, plus extra for
    garnish

3 Tbsp chopped fresh
    tarragon or 2 tsp dried

Kosher salt and freshly
    ground pepper

3 Tbsp pure Canadian maple
    syrup

SERVES 6

I am a huge fan of mushrooms of all types, wild and culti-vated. This dish can stand alone as a side, be used as a pasta sauce, or be turned into a quiche. You might wonder why I use maple syrup with mushrooms; it's an odd combination, but a brilliant one. The maple syrup together with the mush-rooms produces an almost mysterious sweetness that is hard to pinpoint. Go ahead, give this a go; you will love it.

-----

1 Place the dried mushrooms in a bowl and pour 2 cups of hot water over top. Let them soak as long as possible; this can be done at least 2 hours before you proceed with the recipe. The soaking reconstitutes the mushrooms; the longer they sit, the bigger they become.

2 Place the butter in a large sauté pan over medium heat, add the shallots and leek, and sauté until soft, but not brown, about 5 to 7 minutes. Add the garlic, chili paste, and stock paste; stir to dissolve and warm through.

3 Add the fresh mushrooms to the pan and turn the heat to medium-high. Toss the mushrooms in the pan, add the wine, and continue to cook until all of the moisture released from the mushrooms has evaporated, about 10 minutes. While the mushrooms are cooking, drain the soaking mushrooms and squeeze them hard to rid them of any excess water. Chop and add to the pan.

4 Once all the moisture is cooked away, add the cream, parsley, and tarragon, and cook until the sauce has thick-ened, about 5 to 7 minutes. Stir and season with salt and pepper to taste. You can prepare the dish to this point and set aside until serving.

5 Just before you are ready to serve, heat through and driz-zle the maple syrup over top. Stir and transfer to your serving bowl. Garnish with more parsley and serve hot.

NOTE
To use this as a pasta sauce, increase the whipping cream
to 1 cup, heat through, and complete the rest of the recipe.
Pour over hot cooked pasta, toss, and serve.

Sweet Potato Mash

INGREDIENTS

2 lb sweet potatoes or yams

Kosher salt

½ cup sour cream

3 Tbsp balsamic vinegar

2 Tbsp freshly grated
   Parmesan cheese

2 Tbsp unsalted butter

Sea salt and freshly ground
   pepper

⅓ cup chopped toasted
   pecans (optional garnish;
   see page 166)

SERVES 6

Photo on previous page

The tart yet sweet addition of balsamic vinegar lifts the humble sweet potato to new heights. The choice of sweet potato versus yam is personal. I like sweet potatoes for their color, and they are readily available in every market, making this side dish even easier to prepare.

1 Peel and cut the sweet potatoes into sixths. Place in a pot and add water to cover the potatoes. Salt the water, cover, and boil until tender or a fork can easily pierce through, about 12 to 15 minutes. Drain well.

2 Return the drained sweet potatoes to the same pot. Add the sour cream, balsamic, Parmesan, and butter. Using an immersion blender or an electric hand mixer, purée the potatoes until creamy and smooth. Alternatively, you can use a food processor; just ensure the potatoes are lump-free and creamy. Season to taste with salt and pepper. Transfer to a serving bowl and garnish with the pecans, if using.

NOTE

If you want to take this one step further, transfer the puréed mixture into a piping bag fitted with a large star tip. Pipe large rosettes onto a parchment-lined cookie sheet; you should have about six rosettes, or more if you prefer them smaller. Set aside until ready to serve. When you are ready, heat the oven to broil. Set the cookie sheet in the oven and let the rosettes brown; watch attentively, as they will brown fairly quickly. Remove with a flat spatula and transfer them to your serving platter. Garnish with finely chopped parsley if desired.

Savory Zucchini Cakes

It is hard to say no to all your hobby gardener friends who want to heap their homegrown zucchini harvest upon you. Forget the muffins and breads and bring on this savory little fritter that is great as a starter or served as a side dish.

———————

1 Lightly beat the egg in a large bowl. Add the crumbled feta, shallot, dill, and mint. Add in the squeezed grated zucchini and stir to combine. Add the panko crumbs and combine. The mixture should not be soupy; if there is a lot of moisture, add a bit more panko crumbs. Season with salt and pepper to taste. Scoop golf ball-sized portions of the zucchini mixture and form into uniform patties. Set aside.

2 Mix together the sour cream and horseradish (to taste) and set aside.

3 Heat a nonstick fry pan on medium-high heat, and add a teaspoon of olive oil to the pan. Working in batches, fry the zucchini cakes until golden brown on both sides, about 5 minutes per side. Transfer to a tray lined with paper towel to absorb any excess oil. You will have to add a tiny bit of oil to the pan for each batch.

4 Serve with horseradish cream and tiny sprigs of dill, if using.

INGREDIENTS

1 large free-range egg

1 cup crumbled feta cheese

2 Tbsp finely minced shallot

1 Tbsp chopped fresh dill

2 tsp chopped fresh mint

1 large zucchini, skin on, grated using the medium shred, and moisture squeezed out (about 2 cups grated; see note)

1 cup panko crumbs

Sea salt and freshly ground pepper

⅔ cup sour cream

1 to 2 Tbsp horseradish

Olive oil, for frying (any kind works here)

Dill sprigs (optional garnish)

MAKES 20 CAKES

Photo on next page

NOTE
The easiest method for squeezing out the water from grated zucchini is to place the grated zucchini in the center of a clean tea towel. Bring the edges up to meet the middle and wring it hard. Voilà, moisture gone. Alternatively, squeeze really hard with your bare hands. Either way, this is a super-important step.

Yukon Smashed Potatoes

This is truly the easiest preparation for potatoes. I like to use the small nugget size for two reasons: they crisp up quickly and serving is so easy, almost like finger food. Don't be stingy with your portions; you will be surprised at how fast they vanish.

———

1 Preheat your oven to 400°F.

2 Bring a large pot of water to boil, add the kosher salt, and drop in the potatoes.

3 Cook the potatoes until a knife easily pierces through them, about 8 to 10 minutes. Do not undercook, or they will resist smashing. Remove from the heat and drain. Let them cool until you can easily handle them.

4 Transfer the potatoes to a cookie sheet in a single layer. Place a heavy, flat-bottomed drinking cup on top of a potato, then push down to break the skin and smash the potato flat. Repeat for the remaining potatoes. Take care to apply pressure evenly so that they are evenly crushed.

5 Drizzle about 1 teaspoon of olive oil over each potato and top with a sprinkle of fleur de sel. Bake in the oven for 30 minutes, or until the potatoes are crispy and brown. Serve hot.

INGREDIENTS

Kosher salt

2 lb nugget Yukon potatoes, whole (do not peel or cut)

½ cup extra virgin olive oil (approximately)

Fleur de sel (see note)

SERVES 6

NOTES

For a twist, try putting a teaspoon-sized piece of Gorgonzola in the center of each potato 10 minutes before they come out of the oven. Do not add the cheese too early, as it will just ooze out.

You can also switch out the fleur de sel for truffle salt to give the potatoes some importance.

Jacket Roasted Sweet Potatoes with Herbed Feta and Chorizo

INGREDIENTS

3 medium sweet potatoes, scrubbed

1 stick (about 4 oz) cured spicy chorizo, thinly sliced and julienned

1 cup crumbled feta cheese

⅓ cup chopped fresh parsley

⅓ cup chopped fresh cilantro

4 Tbsp sour cream

4 Tbsp Greek yogurt

1 tsp fresh lemon zest

Freshly ground pepper

Chili flakes (garnish)

Julienned lemon zest (garnish)

SERVES 6

This is not your old-school, pedestrian baked potato; I have taken it up a notch by using sweet potatoes and garnishing them with creamy herbed feta and chorizo. Bring it on! For a vegetarian option, omit the chorizo.

---

1 Preheat your oven to 350°F.

2 Place the potatoes directly on the oven rack and bake for about 40 minutes, or until they are soft when you squeeze them.

3 While the potatoes are baking, dry-fry the chorizo in a fry pan over medium heat until it is crispy on both sides, about 10 minutes total. Blot on paper towel to remove any excess oil, then set aside.

4 Place the feta, parsley, cilantro, sour cream, yogurt, and lemon zest in the bowl of a food processor and cream the ingredients together.

5 To serve, cut the potatoes in half and give them a squeeze to break the flesh a bit. Place on a serving plate, and evenly divide the feta mixture over the halves. Sprinkle the chorizo over top. Give the potatoes a good grinding of pepper and top each with a pinch of chili flakes to taste and a sprinkle of julienned lemon zest.

Hasselback Potatoes

This fanned potato hails from Sweden. The concept is not only easy, but unique, prompting the question, "why didn't I think of that?" Simply put, you cut slices into peeled potatoes without cutting completely through. This is accomplished by purchasing an inexpensive hasselback tray (see page 7), or by laying the potato on a large wooden spoon or two chopsticks, which prevents the knife from slicing through. The options for stuffing them from there are endless; I use lemon, thyme, and Asiago in this version.

INGREDIENTS

6 medium Yukon gold or
    russet potatoes, peeled
Extra virgin olive oil, for
    brushing
2 lemons, thinly sliced
12 sprigs fresh thyme
Fleur de sel and freshly
    ground pepper
1 cup grated Asiago cheese

SPECIAL EQUIPMENT
Hasselback tray (see page 7)

MAKES 6 POTATOES

1 Preheat your oven to 375°F.

2 Carefully slice off about ¾ inch from the bottom of the potato to enable it to lie flat. Lay the potato on the hasselback tray and make a cut every ¼ inch along the entire length of the potato. Repeat with the remaining potatoes.

3 Brush the potatoes with oil, making sure you get in between each slice. Place a slice of lemon in every other slit, alternating with sprigs of thyme, then top with a good sprinkle of fleur de sel and a grind of pepper.

4 Bake in the oven for 45 minutes. Remove, distribute the Asiago over each potato, turn the oven down to 350°F, and bake for another 10 minutes or until the cheese is bubbly and golden brown. Serve hot.

Sweet Potato Fries

INGREDIENTS

6 large sweet potatoes

½ cup olive oil (any kind works here)

2 Tbsp grey salt or Maldon salt (see note)

Freshly ground pepper

Chipotle mayo or spicy ketchup, for dipping

SERVES 4 TO 6

I confess that fries are my complete and total weakness. Honestly, who can really resist a mountain of crispy sweet potatoes, roasted deep, dark brown and screaming to be dipped into a chipotle mayo or spicy ketchup? Not me!

---

1 Preheat your oven to 400°F.

2 Peel the sweet potatoes and trim any blemishes. If you like the skin, keep it on; just wash the potatoes well.

3 Cut the potatoes into matchstick pieces, about ¼- to ½-inch thick to suit your preference. The thinner they are, the crispier they will be. Place the sticks in a large bowl and pour the oil over top. Use your hands to toss to ensure all surfaces are glistening with oil.

4 Lay the fries on a parchment-lined cookie sheet in a single layer; ensuring that they are not stacked will encourage even browning. Sprinkle with your salt of choice and roast in the oven for about 30 minutes, depending on size; the thinner they are, the quicker they will cook. Turn them every 10 minutes, moving the fries on the outside edge to the middle so they all cook evenly. Season with freshly ground pepper to taste, and serve hot with chipotle mayo or spicy ketchup.

NOTE

Maldon salt, from Essex, is a large-flake pure salt. Grey salt is from Normandy and is larger and grainier. Grey is particularly perfect for things like focaccia and potatoes when you want to have bits of salt on your food, as it does not melt immediately.

Better than Pad Thai

INGREDIENTS

3 Tbsp roasted grapeseed oil

1 heaping cup sliced yellow onion

10 large shiitake or white button mushrooms, julienned

2 large cloves garlic, minced

1 package (8 oz) thin rice noodles

3 cups finely shredded napa cabbage

2 cups snap peas, strings removed and halved

Ten years ago, I tasted a version of pad Thai in, of all places, Frankfurt, Germany. I loved its depth of flavor, but dismissed the inclusion of pork fat. Instead, I opt here for a spicy vegetarian version that in my opinion is also a perfect side for grilled chicken, prawns, or pork tenderloin.

---

1 Mix all of the sauce ingredients together, and set aside.

2 Heat a wok or large fry pan on medium-high heat, add the grapeseed oil, and toss in the onion. Let the onion sauté to dark brown, about 15 minutes, then add the mushrooms and garlic. Cook until the mushrooms and garlic are browned, about 8 to 10 minutes, stirring occasionally.

3 Meanwhile, soak the noodles in hot water until just soft, about 10 to 15 minutes, taking care not to oversoak them. Drain well.

4 Add the remaining vegetables to the onion, mushroom and garlic mixture, and continue to toss until the cabbage is wilted and all the other vegetables are al dente, about 6 to 8 minutes.

5 Add the drained noodles to the pan along with the sauce. Maintain the heat at medium-high and toss well to combine all the ingredients evenly. Remove from heat, turn the pad Thai out onto a large serving platter and garnish with the chopped nuts and herbs.

6 spears asparagus, tough ends removed and cut into 2-inch pieces

1 medium carrot, peeled and julienned

1 medium red pepper, julienned

1 stalk celery, sliced thin on the diagonal

⅔ cup coarsely chopped cashews or peanuts (garnish)

1 heaping cup coarsely chopped fresh cilantro (garnish)

½ cup coarsely chopped fresh mint (garnish)

SAUCE

2 Tbsp soy sauce

2 Tbsp oyster sauce

2 Tbsp chili paste (see page 4)

1 Tbsp grated ginger (see note, page 94)

1 heaping Tbsp fresh lime zest

1 Tbsp fresh lime juice

1 Tbsp toasted sesame oil (see page 5)

2 tsp rice vinegar

SERVES 6 TO 8

Lemony Risotto

4 cups chicken or vegetable
   stock

3 Tbsp unsalted butter

1 large shallot, finely minced

1 cup arborio rice

½ cup dry white wine

3 Tbsp freshly grated
   Parmesan cheese

2 tsp fresh lemon zest

1 Tbsp fresh lemon juice

¼ cup finely minced Italian
   parsley (garnish)

Freshly ground pepper

SERVES 6

You cannot make risotto with just any rice. It must be arborio rice from the Po Valley in Italy, a short-grain rice that has the unique ability to absorb warm liquid (stock) as it's stirred and cooked. The secret to perfect risotto is slow cooking in a wide, shallow pan and adding the hot stock ½ cup at a time. You must never rush risotto; you wait for it, it never waits for you. The bright, clean flavor infusion of fresh lemon zest and juice gives this side a lovely taste that lingers.

---

1 Place the stock in a saucepan and bring to a low boil, then turn it down to a steady simmer for the duration of the cooking process.

2 Melt 2 Tbsp of the butter in a high-sided 3-quart saucepan, add the shallot, and turn the heat to medium-low. Cook the shallot until soft, but not brown, about 6 minutes. Add the rice and continue to stir until the rice turns translucent, about 5 minutes. Once the rice turns, add the wine all at once. The mixture will sizzle and absorb the wine within a minute or so.

3 Thus begins the love affair with you and risotto. Add ½ cup hot stock to the rice, stirring the entire time as the stock is absorbed into the rice. Continue adding stock ½ cup at a time and stirring until the rice is creamy and cooked through. This process should take about 30 to 40 minutes.

4 Once the risotto is cooked to your preference (some like it more al dente than others), stir in the Parmesan, remaining butter, and lemon zest and juice. Transfer to your serving dish and sprinkle with the parsley and pepper to taste.

NOTE

I love serving this as a bed for grilled fish; it is a perfect marriage.

Spaghetti Carbonara

This is one of those rushed, last-minute "I need a pasta fix" recipes. It packs flavor, and all the ingredients are generally on hand. I always keep a dozen or so sticks of cured chorizo in my freezer. My go-to is, without a doubt, the spicy Spanish version from Oyama Sausage Co. on Granville Island in Vancouver. It is lean, gutsy, and what I call "adult candy." If Oyama is not in your area, use your favorite type of chorizo. To keep it meat-free, just eliminate the chorizo.

---

1 In a large fry pan, dry-fry the chorizo over medium heat until it is crispy on both sides, about 10 minutes total. Transfer to a paper-towel-lined plate to absorb any excess oil. Set aside.

2 In the same pan, add the olive oil, shallot, and garlic. Maintain the heat on medium, and cook the mixture until soft but not brown, about 3 to 4 minutes. Remove from heat and set aside.

3 Bring a large pot of salted water to a boil, add the spaghetti, and cook, according to package instructions, until al dente.

4 While the pasta is cooking, mix the cream cheese, egg, and lemon juice together until combined. If using chili paste, add it here.

5 Drain the pasta, reserving ¼ cup of the pasta water. Add the drained pasta to the shallot pan along with the reserved pasta water and the cream cheese mixture. With the heat on medium, toss to coat the noodles, then add the chorizo and the Parmesan cheese.

6 Transfer to a serving bowl and sprinkle with the parsley, basil, and chili flakes, if using. Finish with a sprinkle of fleur de sel and ground pepper to taste.

INGREDIENTS

1 stick (about 4 oz) cured spicy chorizo, thinly sliced and julienned
1 Tbsp extra virgin olive oil
1 large shallot, finely minced
2 large cloves garlic, minced
Kosher salt
4 portions (10 oz) spaghetti
½ cup full-fat plain cream cheese, room temperature
1 large free-range egg, lightly beaten
Juice of ½ small lemon
1 tsp chili paste (optional; see page 4)
⅓ cup freshly grated Parmesan cheese
¼ cup finely chopped fresh parsley
¼ cup finely chopped fresh basil, plus extra for garnish
1 tsp chili flakes (optional)
Fleur de sel and freshly ground pepper

SERVES 4

Photo on page 122

Ruth's Truffle Pasta

INGREDIENTS

Kosher salt

1 package (8.8 oz) egg pappardelle

Extra virgin olive oil, for drizzling

¼ cup unsalted butter

2 large shallots, finely minced

2 small cloves garlic, minced

1 cup whipping cream (33%)

1 jar (5.6 oz) black truffle spread (I like La Madia La Tartufata Black Truffle Spread & Topping)

Sea salt and freshly ground pepper

Few drops of truffle oil

½ cup freshly grated Parmesan cheese

⅓ cup finely chopped parsley (garnish)

SERVES 6

Ruth Grierson has been cooking with me for well over 25 years. We will leave it at that, as it could easily be longer! Her extensive knowledge in the kitchen has been a tremendous asset over the years. The Gourmet Warehouse sponsors a charity event every year called the Chocolate Challenge, where we host award-winning chocolatiers and food stations for the guests. This dish was Ruth's creation for the 2015 event.

———————————

1 In a large pot of boiling salted water, cook the pasta, according to package instructions, until al dente. Drain, drizzle a little olive oil over to prevent it from sticking, and set aside.

2 Melt the butter in a sauté pan. Add the shallots and garlic, and cook until they are soft but not brown, about 5 to 7 minutes. Add the cream and bring the sauce to a boil to reduce the volume by a third, about 10 minutes. Stir in the black truffle spread and season with sea salt and pepper to taste.

3 Add a few drops of truffle oil, but be careful, as it is very strong; more is not better. Finish with the Parmesan and stir to combine. Add the cooked pasta to the pan and coat evenly. Transfer to a serving dish and garnish with the chopped parsley. Serve hot.

Angel Hair Pasta with Grape Tomatoes

INGREDIENTS

4 large cloves garlic, minced

5 cups grape tomatoes, halved (preferably assorted colors)

1 heaping cup finely chopped fresh parsley

⅔ cup extra virgin olive oil (see note)

Fleur de sel and freshly ground pepper

Kosher salt

1 lb angel hair pasta

1 heaping cup fresh basil chiffonade (see note, page 66)

1 Tbsp chili flakes (optional)

1 heaping cup fresh Parmesan cheese shavings (garnish)

SERVES 6

Photo on page 122

This deliciously easy side dish is one you will make over and over again. It is a perfect complement to any main that needs a carb side. I promise you, this will be the first plate to disappear every time you serve it.

———————

1 Place the minced garlic in a bowl. Add the tomatoes, parsley, and oil, and fleur de sel and pepper to taste. Mix well and cover with plastic wrap. Let the mixture sit at room temperature for at least 2 to 3 hours for the flavors to infuse. Give it a stir every hour or so.

2 When you are ready to eat, bring a large pot of salted water to boil and add the pasta. Cook according to package instructions, being mindful not to overcook; angel hair takes only minutes. When the pasta is cooked, drain well but do not rinse.

3 Place the pasta in a large serving bowl. Add the reserved tomato mixture, the basil, and the chili flakes, if using. Toss to combine, taste for seasoning, and adjust if needed. Top with a good amount of shaved Parmesan cheese, and serve immediately.

NOTE

I recommend using a high-quality olive oil in this recipe, as it is a main ingredient.

Penne Arrabbiata My Way

I have long been a fan of the gutsy arrabbiata sauce, which is the opposite of the boring, lackluster, ho-hum sauces that play it safe. I am all about that Southern Italian fiery flavor. Here is my 30-minute version! Never dismiss the art of simple combined with spice.

---

1 Bring a large pot of salted water to a boil. Add the penne and cook, according to package instructions, until it is al dente. Once cooked, reserve ¼ cup of the pasta water. Drain the pasta, drizzle a little olive oil over to prevent it from sticking, and set aside.

2 In a large fry pan over medium heat, heat 1 Tbsp of the oil, then add the pancetta, shallot, garlic, and anchovy paste. Sauté until the pancetta begins to crisp and the shallot is golden, about 5 to 7 minutes.

3 Add the tomatoes, tomato sauce, chili paste, and thyme, and stir. Cover and turn down to a simmer. Once the cherry tomatoes have softened and the sauce is cohesive, stir in the reserved pasta water, parsley, and basil. Season to taste with sea salt and freshly ground pepper.

4 Ladle the cooked pasta into the sauce and stir to coat. Transfer to a serving bowl and garnish with a generous amount of Parmesan cheese. Serve hot.

INGREDIENTS

Kosher salt

2 cups penne pasta

1 Tbsp extra virgin olive oil, plus extra for drizzling

½ cup diced Italian pancetta

1 small shallot, finely minced

1 large clove garlic, minced

2 tsp anchovy paste

12 grape tomatoes, halved

⅓ cup tomato sauce

2 to 3 Tbsp chili paste (see page 4)

2 sprigs fresh thyme, leaves only

¼ cup chopped fresh parsley

¼ cup chopped fresh basil

Sea salt and freshly ground pepper

⅔ cup freshly grated Parmesan cheese (garnish)

SERVES 4

Photo on page 122

Four-Cheese Mac and Cheese

I created this recipe for a charity dinner that I cooked at Ronald McDonald House. A community of chefs and volunteers came together to bring a few rays of happiness to families hoping for cures. Comfort was the word of the day, so there was no need for fancy pasta shapes; classic elbow macaroni is the shape of comfort. I also cheesed it up to give a little twist to the classic.

INGREDIENTS

Kosher salt

1 lb elbow macaroni

Extra virgin olive oil, for drizzling

3 Tbsp unsalted butter

3 Tbsp unbleached all-purpose flour

1 cup 2% or whole milk

1 cup mascarpone cheese (see note)

1 cup grated cheddar cheese

1 cup grated fontina cheese

2 Tbsp Dijon mustard

Sea salt and freshly ground pepper

1 ½ cups freshly grated Parmesan cheese

SERVES 6

1 Preheat your oven to 325°F.

2 In a large pot of boiling salted water, cook the pasta, according to package instructions, until al dente. Drain, then drizzle a little olive oil over the pasta to prevent it from sticking.

3 In a medium pot over medium heat, melt the butter, then add the flour and whisk for about 4 minutes to cook out the raw taste of the flour. Slowly whisk in the milk, making sure it is smooth and creamy. Add the mascarpone, cheddar, fontina, and mustard. Whisk to combine and season with salt and pepper to taste.

4 Mix in the cooked macaroni and stir. Transfer to a large ovenproof gratin dish or individual ovenproof serving dishes. Top with the Parmesan cheese and bake in the oven for about 15 minutes, or until golden brown. Serve hot.

NOTE

Mascarpone cheese is Italian cream cheese. It is smoother and richer than regular cream cheese, and readily available at Italian delis and good gourmet stores. Do not worry if you can't source it, though; you can substitute with spreadable, room temperature Philadelphia cream cheese. Just be sure to use the full-fat version and not the low-fat or no-fat options.

Staple Recipes

Every good cook should have a small repertoire of staple ingredients that they lean on and use regularly. They add the "za-za-zoom!" to your creations without a lot of work. All of these recipes give an impressive touch to many dishes, but can easily be prepped ahead to save time. Some of them also make great host or hostess gifts. Homemade always tastes best!

Toasted Nuts and Seeds

MAKES ANY AMOUNT

Toasted nuts and seeds are used to finish or complement many of the dishes in this book. Here's a template for how to toast each type so that they are deliciously golden brown and crunchy. These will keep for up to 2 weeks in an airtight container.

---

1 Preheat your oven to the appropriate temperature (see below).

2 Evenly distribute the nuts or seeds on a single layer on a baking sheet, and place in the hot oven. Toast for the approximate amount of time (see below), or until lightly brown and fragrant, shaking the pan occasionally to encourage even browning. (Pine nuts are the most delicate, so watch them carefully!) Remove and let cool.

TIMES AND TEMPERATURES
Almonds: 325°F; about 20 minutes
Hazelnuts: 325°F; about 25 minutes
Pecans: 325°F; about 20 minutes
Pine nuts: 300°F; about 12 to 15 minutes
Pistachios: 325°F; about 15 minutes
Pumpkin seeds: 325°F; about 12 to 15 minutes

Parmesan Tuiles

These cute little crisps look daunting, but they are truly as easy to make as mounding 2 tablespoons of grated Parmesan onto a parchment-lined cookie sheet and baking. You are welcome to add flavors, such as a teaspoon of smoked paprika, a pinch of lemon zest, or cracked pepper. So easy and such impact. What are you waiting for?

INGREDIENTS
1 ½ cups freshly grated
    Parmesan cheese

MAKES 12 TUILES

Photo on page 67

1 Preheat your oven to 375°F.

2 Place 2-tablespoon mounds of cheese on a parchment-lined cookie sheet, ensuring they are evenly spaced. If you wish to add flavor, do so before you bake.

3 Bake for about 5 to 7 minutes. The cheese will melt and spread into a lace-like cookie. Once the tuiles are flat and golden, remove from the oven immediately. At this point they are very malleable, so laying them on a lightly greased rolling pin will result in a half rounded cup; placing them over the bottom of an upturned muffin pan will yield a fully rounded cup. You have a window of about 30 seconds to mold the tuiles; the minute they harden, they will remain firm. These will keep for 3 to 4 days in an airtight container.

Crispy Capers

These are the perfect garnish. It takes seconds to fry them, and even less time to enjoy them!

INGREDIENTS

⅓ cup capers (or whatever amount you require)

1 cup roasted grapeseed oil, for frying

MAKES ⅓ CUP

---

1 Drain the amount of capers that you require. Lay them on paper towel for at least 5 to 6 hours, or ideally overnight. You want to remove every bit of moisture from the capers.

2 Once the capers are dry, place the grapeseed oil in a pan or pot small enough to bring the level of the oil up to about 1 inch, and heat on medium-high heat. Test-fry one caper in the oil. It should sizzle; if it does not, wait until the oil is hotter. Spoon in about 2 teaspoons of capers at a time. They will take about 10 seconds to fry, and will sizzle and open up like flowers.

3 Remove to a paper-towel-lined plate with a slotted spoon and blot dry with more paper towel. The capers are now crunchy crisp and perfect for use as a garnish. They are best made the day of serving, as they will keep for about 12 hours.

Balsamic Glaze

Preparing a balsamic glaze is really as easy as boiling water. Two ingredients, reduce, cool: glaze.

INGREDIENTS

2 cups inexpensive balsamic vinegar

2 Tbsp brown sugar or liquid honey (see note, page 109)

MAKES 1 CUP

---

1 Place the vinegar in a small stainless-steel pot, bring to a boil, then turn down the heat to a simmer. Continue to cook for about 15 minutes, add the sugar or honey, then cook for 5 minutes more. The vinegar will become thick and syrupy. Let it cool. You now have balsamic glaze.

2 This will keep refrigerated for up to 1 month. Use it on salads, as a glaze for chicken, beef, or pork, or as a garnish. I like to store it in a plastic squeeze bottle so it is easy to use.

Fig, Garlic, and Onion Jam

You can easily purchase this condiment at good gourmet stores everywhere, but it is a bit expensive, so you may want to give this recipe a go. All it takes is patience and a bit of time to cara-melize the onions. Making it yourself comes with not only half the price tag, but the pride of a homemade product.

---

1 Heat the oil and butter in a sauté pan over medium heat. Add the onions and garlic and cook, stirring every 5 minutes or so to promote even browning. The process is slow, as you want the mixture to brown, not burn. After 15 minutes the onions should be evenly browned.

2 Stir in the chopped figs, sherry, and balsamic. Keep the heat on medium and stir occasionally to promote even color-ing. Keep stirring at intervals until all the liquid is absorbed and the mixture resembles thick jam, about 15 minutes.

3 Let cool, transfer to a jar and refrigerate for up to 1 week.

INGREDIENTS

4 tablespoons olive oil (any kind works here)

1 tablespoon butter

2 large white onions, thinly sliced

3 large cloves garlic, finely minced

⅓ cup (about 6) dried Mission figs, cut into eighths

¼ cup sherry, port, or Madeira

¼ cup balsamic vinegar

MAKES 1 HEAPING CUP

Crème Fraîche

Crème fraîche is one of those magical ingredients from the masters of classic French cuisine. Unlike other intimidating sauces, crème fraîche is something that home cooks can master just by following the method, so go forth and con-quer the French kitchen—well, at least for this recipe. Crème fraîche is perfect spooned over fruit cobblers, on caviar, or alongside smoked salmon.

INGREDIENTS

1 cup whipping cream (33%)

4 Tbsp sour cream or buttermilk

MAKES 1 CUP

---

1 Combine both ingredients in a glass jar or glass bowl. Let the mixture sit uncovered for at least 12 hours or overnight at room temperature. Once thick, cover and refrigerate. The crème fraîche will keep for up to 1 week in the refrigerator.

Pesto

INGREDIENTS

3 cups stemmed fresh basil
    leaves

3 cloves garlic, peeled

½ cup freshly grated
    Parmesan cheese

⅓ cup pine nuts

2 tsp freshly ground pepper

1 tsp kosher salt

⅔ cup extra virgin olive oil,
    plus more for topping
    and sealing

MAKES 2 CUPS

I know that decent jarred pesto is available in Italian stores everywhere, and to be honest, I always have a jar in my pantry for emergency situations. There is, however, no comparison whatsoever to homemade. Fresh basil whizzed together with classic ingredients creates an infectious, heady aroma in your kitchen that lingers long after you jar and cap it. When the basil is bountiful, give this pesto a go.

1 Place the basil and garlic in the bowl of a food processor. Process for about 15 seconds until it is somewhat puréed. Add the Parmesan, pine nuts, pepper, and salt. Purée until it is a coarse paste, scraping down the sides so no inconsistent pieces remain.

2 With the motor running, slowly pour in the oil. The pesto will thin out the more oil you add, so watch carefully to achieve your desired consistency.

3 Transfer the mixture to jars and float about ⅛ inch of olive oil on the top. This prevents oxidation and keeps the pesto bright green. Lid and refrigerate for up to 7 days.

NOTES

For a flavor change, substitute the basil with 1 cup of sun-dried tomatoes. The only additional step required is to soak the tomatoes in 2 cups of boiling water for 20 minutes to soften them. Drain well and proceed as the method instructs. (If using oil-packed sun-dried tomatoes, simply blot them well before using.)

The pesto can also be frozen for up to 6 months. If freezing, leave ½ inch of room at the top of the jar after floating the olive oil on top.

Acknowledgements

Where to begin. . . . I always find "thank-yous" the most difficult, for no other reason than the word lacks luster and enthusiasm. I am all about enthusiasm.

It all started with one of my very best besties, Robert McCullough, who just happens to be my publisher. It was many years ago, 1998 to be exact, when we met doing a series called *The Girls Who Dish*. We were an instant friendship! He is honest, warm, funny, and engaging, and always calls it exactly like it is. . . . Bobby, I adore you and thank you for everything, especially for your willingness to publish this book! All your fabulous dishes were a bonus.

Computer skills are clearly not my strength, especially "Track Changes." My fabulous assistant Terri Ellsworth kept me on track and on time. Her patience is saintly and her friendship a blessing. Nagging is a bonus.

The sheer magnitude of shopping, prepping, cooking, and styling 80-plus recipes in short order is beyond belief, but the "A-Team" did it. Diane Lawrence, Susan Meister, Doreen Corday, and Sally Elarmo formed the cooking backbone. They stirred, chopped, whisked, roasted, peeled, sautéed, baked, boiled, fried, rolled, and transformed the recipes into edible perfection.

Then, Becky Paris opened her bag of secret tricks, waved her magical food styling wand, and turned the food into culinary beauty.

Janis Nicolay, the brains behind the lens, crouched and climbed into all sorts of positions to get the best light and angle for each plate. Her talent did not end there, as editing and formatting followed to ensure the images you see in this book are true to life and glorious.

I stand and applaud you all with heaps of gratitude and praise, as this massive cook-off was done in four days—albeit with a few adult beverages to assist!

All of the recipes were born in one form or another in my cooking school. The school would not be possible without my amazing sous chef Ruth Grierson, who always manages to make me look good. Amarilde Lourenco has watched and assisted in the transition from idea to recipe (with a few disasters thrown in!).

All of this takes an enormous amount of time away from my store, The Gourmet Warehouse, so to all of my staff who hold the fort in my absence, I thank you.

Special thanks to Elysse Bell and Paige Farrell at Appetite for their patience and belief, as well as to the lovely and talented ladies that have worked behind the scenes: Jennifer Griffiths, for the gorgeous design, and Susan Burns, Kimberlee Hesas, Susan Traxel, Lindsay Paterson, and Lana Okerlund for ensuring that all the picky and necessary details are covered!

Lastly, to my small little family, the Lawrences, the Meisters, and my amazing children, Christina and Jason: you make life worthwhile and cooking for you is my passionate pleasure.

Index